Continuous Improvement By Improving Continuously (CIBIC)

Addressing the Human Factors During the Pursuit of Process Excellence

Continuous Improvement By Improving Continuously (CIBIC)

Addressing the Human Factors During the Pursuit of Process Excellence

F. Allen Davis

CRC Press
Taylor & Francis Group
Boca Raton London New York

CRC Press is an imprint of the
Taylor & Francis Group, an **informa** business
A PRODUCTIVITY PRESS BOOK

CRC Press
Taylor & Francis Group
6000 Broken Sound Parkway NW, Suite 300
Boca Raton, FL 33487-2742

Printed on acid-free paper

International Standard Book Number-13: 978-1-138-74515-5 (Hardback)

Library of Congress Cataloging-in-Publication Data

Names: Davis, Frank A., author.
Title: Continuous improvement by improving continuously (CIBIC) : addressing the human factors during the pursuit of process excellence / Frank A. Davis.
Description: Boca Raton, FL : CRC Press, 2018.
Identifiers: LCCN 2017012463 | ISBN 9781138745155 (hardback : alk. paper)
Subjects: LCSH: Continuous improvement process. | Performance. | Employee motivation. | Quality control.
Classification: LCC TS183 .D39 2018 | DDC 658.5/33--dc23
LC record available at https://lccn.loc.gov/2017012463

**Visit the Taylor & Francis Web site at
http://www.taylorandfrancis.com**

**and the CRC Press Web site at
http://www.crcpress.com**

For M,

A Gift For The Ages

Contents

Executive Summary

In our increasingly complex world, our wants, needs, and problems can be both ever menacing and ever challenging. A burden for some and a curse for others, these wants, needs, and problems can cloud the mind and ravage the spirit. While some face these challenges with action, others choose the path of callous disregard in failing to address what needs to be addressed. And while some of us possess the insight, know-how, and discipline to address these challenges, others lack the cognitive prowess to pursue a better tomorrow. While these challenges are widely faced by individuals, they are also faced by groups and collective interests. While some leading-edge businesses, organizations, and institutions have erected continuous improvement systems that address wants, needs, and problems at the process and systems level, very few have extended this pursuit into the human capital realm, missing out on the opportunity to extend the pursuit of excellence to a much wider demographic. As a result, even in the midst of superior process and systems continuous improvement, the specter of systemic failure still looms largely. It is out of this fear that CIBIC arises. While some accept human capital deficiency as an unavoidable reality, CIBIC practitioners learn that human capital development is a key element of continuous improvement. By promoting a chaos- and gap-eliminating human capital system, CIBIC promotes the creation of outer strength from inner power, thus extending the pursuit of excellence to a much wider demographic. CIBIC, which is an acronym for Continuous Improvement by Improving Continuously, embraces the pursuit of excellence, individually and collectively, through the use of a system that creates excellence-promoting synergies at all levels. This system is designed to be both elegant and comprehensive. For collective interests, CIBIC promotes the pursuit of excellence through the creation of shared values and synergies that promote new efficiencies. For individuals, CIBIC promotes excellence through the creation of excellence-promoting values and practices. By creating synergies between individual and collective interests, CIBIC promotes the common core values and collective synergies that promote the pursuit of excellence at all levels. While discord, conflict, and division plague many interests, unity, synergy, and excellence reign supreme with CIBIC enthusiasts. Through CIBIC, your hopes for a better tomorrow can begin anew today.

CIBIC
Outer Strength From Inner Power

Continuous improvement is the endeavor to promote an optimal reality through sustainable excellence. Although its language may change, its value is always constant.

Chinese	**Japanese**
連續的提高	継続的改善
Liánxù de tígāo	Keizoku-teki kaizen
Russian	**French**
Постоянное совершенствование	Amélioration continue
Latin	**Greek**
Continua emendationem	Συνεχής βελτίωση
	Synechis veltiosi
German	**Korean**
Ständige Verbesserung	지속적인 개선
	Jisogjeog-in gaeseon
Spanish	**Portuguese**
Mejora continua	Melhoria continua

One goal, *three* laws, *five* philosophies, *seven* progressions, and *nine* drivers and qualities.

Sapphires • Composites • Frameworks • Diagrams • Models • Paradigms

Foreword

While preserving, protecting, and defending your values and principles hold great importance, only the pursuit of excellence can turn your hopes and dreams into your realities. A daily endeavor for some and an occasional desire for others, the pursuit of excellence is neither simple nor easy. In the truest sense of the word, excellence is the manifestation of vision, philosophy, and commitment, and not the relationships, size, and seniority that it is often mistaken for. In the absence of vision, philosophy, and commitment, the pursuit of excellence and continuous improvement becomes an impossible dream. Even interests with relationships, size, and seniority are destined to fail in the absence of these three excellence promoters. Ultimately, it is only through your pursuit of excellence and continuous improvement that you can make today's dreams into tomorrow's realities. Like a dynamic duo for change, the pursuit of excellence and continuous improvement are both critical and essential. By vanquishing the challenges that loom in the distance, continuous improvement and excellence promote the progressive actions that guarantee our successful forward pursuits. While the unknowing, unwilling, and unable turn a blind eye to these looming challenges, continuous improvement and excellence promoters always rise to the occasion. Rather than viewing challenges as unavoidable inhibitors of progress, continuous improvement and excellence promoters learn to address these looming challenges systemically and perpetually. The CIBIC system includes an elegant portfolio of performance-enhancing frameworks and methods that meet the needs of excellence enthusiasts. By promoting the pursuit of excellence individually and collectively, CIBIC succeeds where other systems fail. By extending the pursuit of excellence and continuous improvement from a limited pursuit to a comprehensive process, systems, and human capital pursuit, CIBIC extends the pursuit of excellence and continuous improvement to a much wider demographic. For those who embrace this subject matter with an open mind and an imaginative spirit, continuous improvement will become a much easier endeavor, full of the rewards that excellence brings.

Success Is a Journey and Not a Destination.

Arthur Ashe

Author

 **F. Allen Davis** is a successful startup entrepreneur, president of the Horizon Group of Companies, and chief developer of the CIBIC Continuous Improvement System. A Washington, DC native, Frank is a previous William Randolph Hearst Foundation United States Senate Youth Scholar who earned a bachelor's degree in electrical engineering from Bucknell University and a master's degree in business from the University of Alabama at Birmingham. Frank also earned Executive Program credentials from the Tuck School of Business at Dartmouth. During his 20-year professional career with companies including Westinghouse Electric, Honeywell, Invensys, and Johnson Controls, Frank regularly used his acumen to tackle a wide range of unique and challenging issues. As an entrepreneur, Frank has led the Horizon Group during its award-winning and regularly chronicled 15-year run as a leading diversity owned business. Frank's perspective of continuous improvement has been widely embraced in both the business segment and academia. Frank has held numerous Board of Directors positions with both Bucknell University and the University of Alabama at Birmingham and is an active member of the National Minority Supplier Development Council and the Association for Strategic Planning. Frank is currently listed in *Who's Who Among African Americans* and is a recognized successful author.

Common Sense
Is Not So Common.

VOLTAIRE

Nothing Ventured,
Nothing Gained.

BENJAMIN FRANKLIN

It Is Only through Our Inner
Power That We Build Our
Outer Strength.

F. ALLEN DAVIS

Imaginative Solutions
to Complex Problems Solutions
Appear to Be Simple

F. ALLEN DAVIS

Introduction: The Endeavor of Continuous Improvement

Perpetual change and perpetual challenges dominate our world. The realities of today and the possibilities of tomorrow are in a constant state of flux, creating great uncertainty for us all. Although troublesome for some and the source of anguish for others, these uncertainties highlight the importance of continuous improvement at all levels and in all dynamics. It is only through continuous improvement that our hopes become our dreams and our dreams become our realities. Through continuous improvement, our weaknesses become our strengths and our problems become our opportunities. While some view continuous improvement as a limited organizational pursuit, the truly insightful learn otherwise. "When we improve individually, we grow collectively" is the true mantra of continuous improvement. By embracing this mantra, we make the future brighter for us all. While some also view continuous improvement as a spontaneous pursuit, that view is flawed at best. At its foundation, continuous improvement is a continual pursuit that requires good judgment and common sense. These qualities rise from your willingness to embrace the three precursors of continuous improvement. The **first precursor** of continuous improvement is recognizing that only your inner power can promote your true outer strength. When we commit ourselves to the tireless development of our inner attributes, good things invariably happen. The **second precursor** of continuous improvement is embracing the importance of common sense in your forward pursuits. Although intuitive answers to everyday problems are widely prevalent, naivete and the lack of insight lead far too many of us to make decisions that defy rhyme and reason, making true improvement a hit-and-miss endeavor. Further complicating this precursor is the reality that what's common sense for some, may not be common sense for others, and vice versa. The **third precursor** of continuous improvement is recognizing that needless risk often creates needless trauma. When we discount gaps and our chaotic realities, we promote the very trauma that we should generally seek to limit. In the absence of these three precursors, the pursuit of excellence and continuous improvement both wane, promoting the presence of the gaps and chaotic realities that we should always seek to avoid. These harbingers of discord, destroyers of progress, devastators of hope, and extinguishers of dreams have been a stain on society and our collective best interests since the dawn of time. Our disappointments, our deficiencies, our conflicts, and our discords all rise from the bog of this disruptive duo. It is only through continuous improvement that we can render these gaps and chaotic realities irrelevant, insignificant, and inconsequential. While many struggle with this pursuit, others experience great success. Those who succeed learn that the pursuit of excellence and continuous improvement is best pursued at all levels. While many organizations have achieved process and systems excellence in their business endeavors through the use of Kaizen, Lean, Six Sigma, and ISO continuous improvement, efficiency, and quality systems, many have failed at extending this excellence into the human capital realm, thus missing out on an opportunity to extend the full reach of excellence. And while some of these organizations have learned to promote limited human capital continuous improvement to reinforce their continuous improvement, efficiency, and quality initiatives, most stop short of promoting the comprehensive human capital continuous improvement that promotes the pervasive pursuit of excellence. The CIBIC system addresses this disconnect through the use of a McGregor Theory Y[1] compliant seamless approach to continuous improvement. By addressing the limitations of Kaizen, Lean, Six Sigma, and ISO, CIBIC transforms continuous improvement from a limited process and systems endeavor to a comprehensive process, systems, and human capital pursuit. As noble as this pursuit may seem, it is not without its challenges. For some, the lack of insight, commitment, and maturity can turn this pursuit into a daunting endeavor. For countless others, the loss of hope and hopelessness provides an even greater barrier to progress. While recognizing your impediments is a good first step, that recognition alone is not enough. While recognition is indeed a promoter of continuous improvement and excellence, only your tireless and preemptive actions in pursuit of continuous improvement and excellence will alter your destiny. For those who seek this new reality, CIBIC can be a guiding light. CIBIC, while refreshingly new and creatively imaginative, recognizes the contributions of W. Edwards Deming[2] to the pursuit of quality and continuous improvement. Deming was a twentieth-century engineer, statistician, author, lecturer, and management consultant who advanced the pursuit of quality and continuous improvement through his widely recognized principles. These principles, although organizationally brilliant and creatively imaginative, did not address human capital continuous improvement in comprehensive terms, the same limitation that plagues the other continuous improvement, efficiency, and quality systems. This systemic continuous improvement gap, as highlighted in Figure I.1, is elegantly addressed using the comprehensive assortment of frameworks, models, and methods that are elements of the CIBIC system. CIBIC addresses this continuous improvement gap by highlighting a human capital continuous improvement system that simultaneously promotes process and systems continuous improvement.

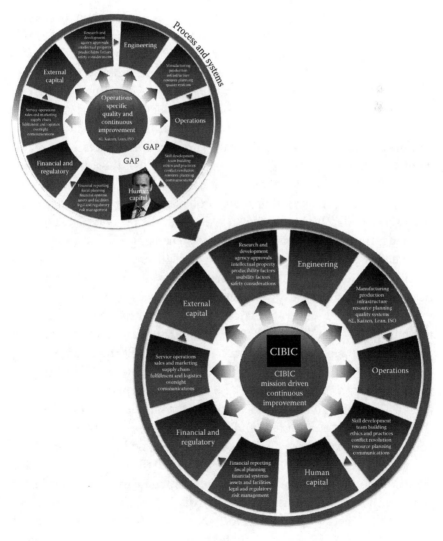

FIGURE I.1
CIBIC comprehensive continuous improvement.

By touting human capital continuous improvement as the essential precursor of process and systems continuous improvement, CIBIC promotes the pursuit of excellence through common sense, sound intuitive decision making, and the tireless pursuit of sustainability. By embracing these qualities enthusiastically, we promote the pursuit of excellence and not the pursuit of mediocrity and failure that plagues far too many, avoiding the poor practices and standards that spawn their existence. These poor practices and standards have laid claim to far too many, extending the reach of misery much further than it needs to extend and promoting the very gaps and chaotic realities that are always best avoided. While these rogue elements can be difficult to identify, address, and eliminate, your effectiveness or lack thereof in eradicating these harbingers of misery will undoubtedly influence your pursuit of excellence and continuous improvement. Those who succeed in this endeavor will promote a better tomorrow, while those who fail face the constant specter of misery, mediocrity, and heartache. By promoting continuous improvement in your individual and collective endeavors, CIBIC helps to eradicate the gaps, chaotic realities, failure, and mediocrity that preclude the pursuit of excellence. For those who embrace CIBIC, life holds infinite potential. Scaling the highest peaks and winning against all odds are all possible, probable, and even likely for CIBIC enthusiasts and CIBIC practitioners. Although the benefits of CIBIC will become intuitively obvious later, outwardly choosing and inwardly deciding to embrace the system is not without its challenges. Conflicting values, conflicting priorities, conflicting interests, and your general chaotic realities can sometimes make the pursuit of excellence an excessively challenging endeavor. And while wisdom, insight, and common sense can make this pursuit an easier endeavor, these qualities are almost always acquired over time through positive exposure and patience. Further complicating this pursuit for some are underlying social, economic, and demographic considerations that can disrupt the bilateral mechanisms for corrective action. These underlying considerations can promote doubt, malaise, disappointment, discouragement, and the general loss of hope that can render your pursuit of excellence doubtful, questionable, and improbable. While the hopeless view life's realities with pessimism, CIBIC enthusiasts learn to view these same realities with optimism. They come to understand that it is in their power to vanquish the doubt, malaise, disappointment, and discouragement that lays claim to far too many. They also come to understand that CIBIC has the power to promote the boundless hopes and unlimited dreams that can fuel a better tomorrow. Although we are each born with the potential to pursue a better tomorrow, many of us fail for tragic reasons. Some of us fail because of a lack of commitment, some as a result of a lack of discipline, some because of a lack of vision, and some are attributed to a wide range of avoidable circumstances, some that we discussed earlier. It is sad that even in the presence of our self-promoted shortcomings, far too many of us still expect a life full of opulence, riches, and fame. Rather than accepting the blame for our self-promoted shortcomings, far too many of us attempt to shift the blame for problems elsewhere, avoiding accountability for our self-promoted shortcomings. While the pursuit of opulence, riches, and fame is a dream for many, only continuous improvement and excellence can truly turn that dream into a reality. And while it is true that the unethical, immoral, unfair, and inconsiderate conduct of others is sometimes at the root of our problems, we must each be willing to nonetheless accept responsibility and accountability, individually and collectively, for the problems and unfavorable realities that we create and control. CIBIC practitioners and CIBIC enthusiasts learn that by actively and sustainably addressing these problems and unfavorable realities through aggressive action, they help to promote a better tomorrow for themselves and others. If you have yet to embrace the nuances of CIBIC, then a new challenge awaits: the challenge of becoming a CIBIC practitioner and CIBIC enthusiast. This challenge begins with a new understanding of the basic elements of CIBIC, including the awareness, preparation, and change subject matters. Although some of this material may seem basic on the surface, as intended, this same material will become more intuitively elegant when considered as part of the grander CIBIC system. For those who come to embrace this system, the resulting lessons learned should be both perspective altering and mentally liberating. By embracing the pursuit of excellence from mediocrity, CIBIC helps to eliminate the waste of potential, waste of material, and waste of time that plagues far too many. While CIBIC is intended to promote life, liberty, and the pursuit of happiness in a manner that is neither overbearing nor unduly restrictive, embracing the system is not always easy. For some, the nuances of CIBIC will be uncomfortable and unsettling to embrace. For others, the required leap of faith will invoke fear and reservations. In most cases, however, any resulting fears and reservations should generally wane with increasing exposure and greater familiarity. It is also important to note that your courage or lack thereof in embracing this subject matter can also influence your level of success. While it is ultimately your choice to be courageous or cowardly in the pursuit of excellence, that choice can have far-reaching consequences and ramifications. However, in the realm of continuous improvement, a brighter future awaits the courageous, while only disappointment looms for the cowardly. We all live in a special window in time, a window in which we have the power to control our destiny through our courage and level of commitment. To not embrace that opportunity is a monumental waste of time and a sad waste of potential. Regardless of your realities, your pursuit of excellence will always begin and end with your discoveries.

1

Discovery

The pursuit of new discoveries and insight can be tiresome, stressful, and insanely thought provoking for many. The burden of information gathering creates challenges for us all. But while discovery and insight can fuel your pursuits, the lack thereof can fuel your woes. And while the pursuit of discovery is critically important, the importance of insight is no less critical. Discovery is the action or process of finding, locating, uncovering, or unearthing new information. In the absence of discovery, developing new insight becomes difficult, arduous, and widely improbable. Insight is the conscious use of discovery to promote the greater recognition, realization, comprehension, and appreciation of a specific body of knowledge. It is only through your discoveries that continuous improvement is possible, and it is only through your insight that excellence can prevail. With all of their co-dependencies and all of their interrelations, discovery and insight are distinctly unique, as shown in Figure 1.1. **Discovery** is built from your interactions, observations, consultations, analysis, determinations, and assessments, hereafter referred to as the six elements of discovery. **Insight**, on the other hand, is built from your *comprehension* of the relativities, contingencies, circumstances, environmental attributes, and values that exist and prevail, hereafter referred to as the six elements of insight. While discovery and insight are distinctly important, their relative importance is equal and balanced. Only discovery can promote your insight, and only your insight can promote your discoveries. While discovery is about the pursuit of information, insight is about the comprehension and interpretation of that information. Your successful use of discovery and insight is first and foremost based on your comprehension of the six elements of discovery and the six elements of insight. Each of the six elements of discovery has a unique importance. Interactions highlight your informal discussions and conversations. Observations highlight your

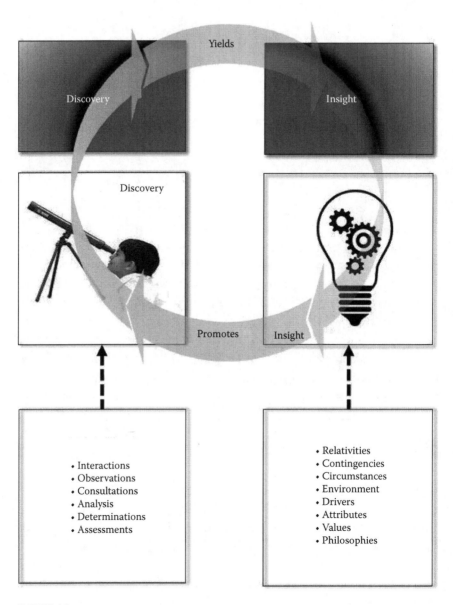

FIGURE 1.1
Discovery and insight.

visual or sensory experiences. Consultations highlight your formal discussions, conversations, and contracted engagements. Analysis highlights your numerical or scientific interpretation of a given set of information. Determination highlights your nonscientific interpretation of a given set of information. And, finally, assessment highlights your general interpretation of primarily qualitative information. Together, these six elements of discovery describe your discovery complex. The six elements of insight have alternately unique importance. Relativities highlight your strengths and weaknesses. Contingencies highlight your opportunities and threats. Circumstances highlight the *specific* conditions that exist. Environment highlights the *wider-scale* conditions that exist. Attributes highlight your prevailing drivers and qualities. And, finally, values highlight the principles and philosophies that exist or are currently being embraced and followed.

In general terms, discovery promotes insight, and insight drives discovery. Before we can pursue continuous improvement and excellence, we must first be willing to embrace the importance of discovery and insight as the initial promoters of progress. While discovery promotes insight, it is ultimately our insight that promotes progress. It is only through insight that we rise, prevail, succeed, and triumph. When insight rises, prosperity grows, but when insight wanes, chaos rises. It is only through our insight that we can vanquish chaos. Like a menacing storm cloud, chaos is ever present, ever menacing, and ever threatening. Crushing in influence and demoralizing in effect, chaos ruins lives, crushes hopes, and extinguishes dreams. From conflict and discord to gridlock and destruction, chaos can wreak widespread havoc and total devastation. It is only through the prevention of chaos that your dreams for tomorrow can become a reality today. But what is chaos? Chaos is the manifestation of the despair, deficiency, and destruction that you experience in your everyday endeavors. While gaps promote chaos, chaos can correspondingly promote gaps. As was the case with discovery and insight, it is only through your understanding of chaos and gaps that the pursuit of excellence is possible. While gaps represent our specific deficiencies, chaos represents our general realities. And whereas gaps are generally easy to grasp, chaos is much harder to classify. Gaps highlight the differences between our current and our desired realities, usually measured qualitatively or quantitatively. While all gaps require your attention, the severity of gaps can vary greatly. While some gaps can spawn chaos, other gaps are nonchaotic and purely attention invoking in nature. When gaps spawn chaos, the urgency of corrective action increases markedly. Chaos, on the other hand, is a much more dynamic subject matter. Chaos is the manifestation of nine dynamics: social, economic, psychological, physiological, environmental, technical, chronological, performance, and biological–chemical–pharmacological dynamics, also referred to as the nine Chaos Designation Types (CDTs) as shown in Figure 1.2. Social chaos highlights those societal realities that affect and otherwise influence our social status, social adaptability, and social awareness. Economic chaos highlights those financial and monetary realities that affect and otherwise influence our standard of living, capital access, capital utilization, investment posture, cost dynamics, and compensation, among others. Physiological chaos highlights those physical realities that affect and otherwise influence our ability to physically meet or exceed a given set of expectations. Psychological chaos highlights those mental, cognitive, intellectual, and neurological realities that affect and otherwise influence our ability to mentally meet or exceed a given set of expectations.

Environmental chaos highlights those earth, air, water, climate, pollution, atmospheric, and toxicology realities that affect and otherwise influence the ability of our planet and our habitat to sustain life and meet or exceed a given set of agreed upon standards for minimum human existence. Technical chaos highlights those usability, convenience, innovative, and design realities that affect and otherwise influence our ability to produce and use tangible and intangible products, systems, services, software, and solutions. Chronological chaos highlights those timing, time span, elapsed time, and time delay realities that impact and otherwise influence our ability to meet or exceed a specific time requirement. Performance chaos highlights those quality, safety, reliability, legality, accuracy, academic achievement, and professional realities that control or otherwise influence our standing versus the prevailing expectations that exist. Bio–chem–pharma chaos highlights the genetic, life safety, pharmacological, chemical, and substance-related realities that control or otherwise influence the nonenvironmental elements of our existence. Within the nine chaos types, the severity and significance of chaos can vary. While some view chaos in absolute terms, the severity of chaos can vary greatly. The Chaos Severity Level (CSL) classifies chaos in one of three levels: despair, deficiency, and destruction levels. **Despair,** the first and most acute level of chaos, is described by the active presence of irritation, inconvenience, and general concern. While despair may be viewed by many as an unavoidable life circumstance, the reality is that its existence is often a gateway enabler for more invasive and severe levels of chaos. **Deficiency,** the second and

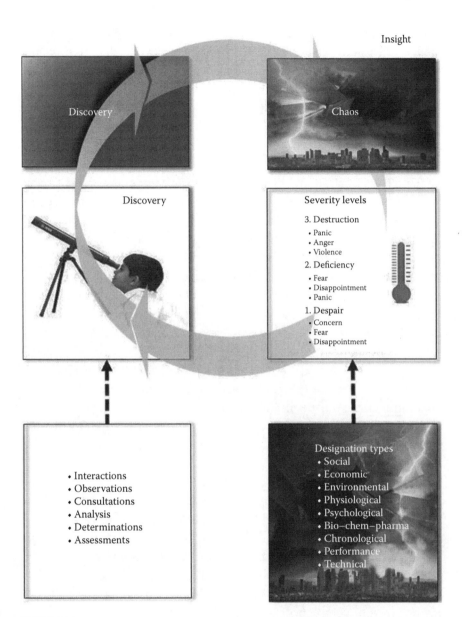

FIGURE 1.2
Chaos types and severity levels.

mid-level form of chaos, is described by the active presence of waste and inefficiency as promoted by the widespread deficiencies that exist. While waste and inefficiency may be accepted by many as a general norm, the reality is that these antagonists introduce sometimes critical consequences into what was previously an acceptable scenario. The deficiencies that exist can often promote the onset of fear, disappointment, and sometimes panic depending on the specific scenario. **Destruction**, the third and most severe form of chaos, is described by the active presence of tangible and intangible devastation and loss as created by the widespread destruction that exists. Although terrorists, hoodlums, criminals, and miscreants may embrace destruction as a facilitating pursuit, the conscientious and generally responsible among us recognize that devastation and loss are generally best avoided. Together with the CDTs, the three levels of chaos help describe chaos in generally more comprehensible terms. While gap responsibility, accountability, solvability, and preventability (GRASP) can eliminate gaps at the fundamental level, only the comprehensive CIBIC system can simultaneously eliminate gaps, chaos, and chaotic realities at both the singular and collective levels. Be it due to limited awareness, lack of control, callous disregard, lack of influence, poor risk management, or self-serving biases, the existence of gaps and chaotic realities need not be the promoter of your demise if you embrace CIBIC as your mechanism for change. And while you may be fully committed to change, it is important for you to recognize that on occasion, change may be out of your control. Renowned American theologian, ethicist, and public intellectual Reinhold Niebuhr once famously said "God grant me the serenity to accept the things I cannot change, the courage to change the things I can, and the wisdom to know the difference." Niebuhr's quote truly applies to the realities that you may face during your pursuit of a better tomorrow. While we each respond to fear, anxiety, stress, failure, and loss differently, it is ultimately your willingness to face these specters head on that will determine your level of success or lack thereof. That pursuit will always begin with your comprehension of the CIBIC system.

The Task of Art Today Is to Bring Chaos into Order.

THEODOR ADORNO

God Grant me the Serenity to Accept the Things I cannot Change, the Courage to Change the Things I can, and the Wisdom to Know the Difference.

REINHOLD NIEBUHR

2

The System

Now that you have newfound awareness and a better understanding of the dynamics of discovery, a new challenge awaits: the challenge of using these new discoveries to promote your pursuit of excellence. That challenge, although easy sounding, is anything but easy. Even the most experienced people struggle with the burden of finding the right path forward for a given set of circumstances. And while desire and motivation can aid you in this pursuit, that desire and motivation is useless in the absence of vision and structure. Since the dawn of time, men and women alike have struggled with the burden of making the right decisions and choosing the right path forward. The dynamic and ever-changing nature of the world invariably creates cognitive challenges for individuals, groups, and collective interests. While some have sought out the solace of the spiritual realm, others have sought out nontraditional approaches to guide their forward pursuits. Although our spirituality feeds the soul, only our practicality can drive our pursuit of excellence. In continuous improvement, our practicality rises from the systems that promote change and an optimal existence. In the CIBIC system, true excellence and continuous improvement both rise from the frameworks, models, and methods that comprise the system. These system elements promote the pursuit of excellence from mediocrity using anti-chaotic standards and practices. At the heart of the CIBIC system is the comprehensively elegant EDGE framework. EDGE, which is an acronym for Efficient and Detailed Gap Elimination, highlights the success in promoting elements at a fundamental level. Superficially, EDGE highlights the huge fundamental importance of planning and action as promoters of continuous improvement as highlighted in Figure 2.1. EDGE also promotes the leveraging of awareness, preparation, and change as facilitators of excellence. At the actionable level, the EDGE framework emphasizes the importance of exposure, discovery, insight, configuration,

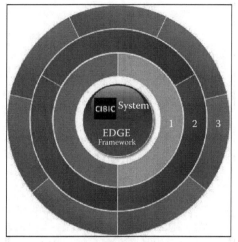

Vision

Aggressively pursue excellence and continuous improvement using a new seamless and scalable three-level system that promotes rapid affinity and use.

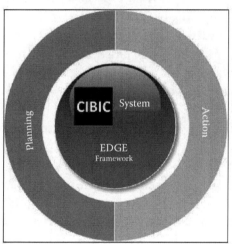

Level 1 Structure

Promote this pursuit using a three-level hemispheric model that emphasizes the dual importance of planning and action as precursors for change. This structure highlights the inherent codependency of planning and action in continuous improvement and the pursuit of excellence, the precise being that planning without action is just as bad as action without planning.

FIGURE 2.1
The EDGE framework basic structure.

development, deployment, and continuation as promoters of excellence as shown in Figure 2.2. The **exposure** phase, which we discussed earlier, highlights the process of developing a superficial understanding of the prevailing conditions that exist in general terms. The **discovery** phase highlights the development of a basic understanding of the prevailing circumstances, objectives, values, and environment that exist either individually or collectively. The **insight** phase, which we also discussed earlier, highlights the importance of investigation, research, due diligence, fact

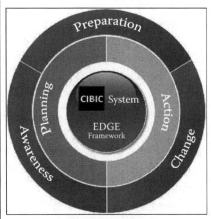

Framework

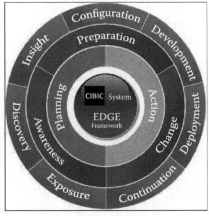

Level 2 Structure
The EDGE level 2 structure expands on the level one model by refining the planning and action continuous improvement elements into the more descriptive and actionable awareness, preparation, and change elements.

Level 3 Structure
The EDGE level 3 structure further expands on the EDGE level 1 and level 2 models by highlighting the seven definitive actionable phases of continuous improvement:

Exposure
Superficial awareness.

Discovery
Building a basic understanding of the specific performance, societal, learning, or resource management dynamics that exist.

Insight (building)
Developing an enhanced qualitative and quantitative understanding of the specific performance, societal, learning, or resource management dynamics that exist.

Configuration
The process of developing a basic plan for the successful use of drivers, attributes, qualities, competencies, and resources to promote continuous improvement and the pursuit of excellence.

Development
The development of drivers, attributes, qualities, competencies, and resources to promote continuous improvement and the pursuit of excellence.

Deployment
The planned use of drivers, attributes, qualities, competencies, and resources to promote continuous improvement and the pursuit of excellence.

Continuation
The sustainability of a chosen course of action.

FIGURE 2.2
The EDGE framework and expanded structure.

finding, counseling, assessments, and specific information gathering in the overall pursuit of excellence and continuous improvement. This phase includes building a very specific understanding of the prevailing gaps and chaotic realities that exist.

Although blindly focusing on the use of your strongest quality or competency may be appealing to you personally, the truly successful learn to use those qualities and competencies in a manner that is appropriate for their given circumstances. The **configuration** phase highlights the process of focusing your key attributes to promote the pursuit of change. This phase emphasizes the systemic use of your collective attributes to address, resolve, or negate the gap, deficiency, and chaotic circumstances that may exist for you individually, collectively, or organizationally. The fifth phase, the **development** phase, highlights the critical need for focused development as a precursor of change. The development phase emphasizes the need for the sustained development of your inner drivers and outer qualities as a precursor to the pursuit of excellence. The sixth phase of **deployment** highlights the direct use of drivers, attributes, qualities, competencies, and resources to create the forward progress that promotes continuous improvement and the pursuit of excellence. And finally, the seventh and final phase of continuation highlights the systemic need for follow through and sustainability to promote excellence and continuous improvement. Together, these seven phases promote the tireless pursuit of excellence and continuous improvement that promote your optimal realities. By repeating the EDGE cycle ad infinitum, you develop the inertia and momentum to continue this chosen pursuit indefinitely. While different endeavors require a differing number of EDGE phases, wise practitioners learn that the use of all seven EDGE phases typically yields the best results. These same skilled practitioners learn to recognize the great systemic importance of the configuration phase. The configuration phase lies at the junction of the awareness and change phases. While some discount the role of configuration, its importance is truly undeniable. In the configuration phase, the insight yielded from the awareness phase is used to structure and promote the development and deployment phases. This direct action is driven by the recognition, comprehension, and active use of your inner and outer attributes, referred to in the CIBIC system as your inner drivers and outer qualities. The inner drivers represent the nine critical inner attributes while the outer qualities represent the nine critical outer attributes. The nine outer qualities represent the nine outer attributes that control, influence, and facilitate your tangible worldly pursuit of continuous improvement and sustainability as visible to the outside world. Systemically speaking, inner driver development promotes outer qualities strength, and vice versa. In the absence of the nine outer qualities, continuous improvement, sustainability, and the pursuit of excellence all become virtual impossibilities, greatly diminishing your hopes for tomorrow. Although we will cover the nine inner drivers and nine outer qualities in later chapters, I will introduce them to you now for continuity purposes. The nine inner drivers are stability, adaptability, planning, patience, humility, intelligence, resilience, enthusiasm, and sustainability.

The nine outer qualities are convenience, opinions, motivations, proficiency, output, sustainability, influences, timeliness, and economics. These inner drivers, outer qualities, and their illustrative visuals, which we will discuss more in the coming chapters, are highlighted in Figure 2.3. As you should undoubtedly observe in this book and in your practical applications, these inner drivers and outer qualities truly play a major role in your excellence-based pursuits. As you become more skilled in recognizing their influence, you should develop a heightened awareness of just

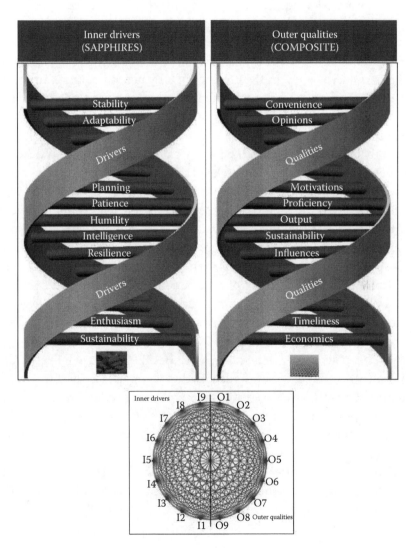

FIGURE 2.3
Your DNA—the inner drivers and outer qualities.

how important these drivers and qualities are in the comprehension of world dynamics and your specific realities. As you will discover in greater detail later, the CIBIC system also includes a variety of Performance Tools that are specifically designed to support your awareness, preparation, and change endeavors in a manner that supports long-term use and retention. The creatively designed retention features are designed to promote your efficient and sustained use of the comprehensive system while also creating the process driven elegance that promotes your pursuit of excellence. Like a modern-day symphony, this process-driven elegance is both anti-chaotic and pro-harmonic. Renowned physicists, mathematicians, and composers from Albert Einstein to Wolfgang Amadeus Mozart have used elegance as the central foundation of their creative pursuits since the dawn of modern times. In the presence of elegance, our spirit is stronger, our vision is clearer, our commitment is more resolute, and our senses are more refined. Through our elegance, we can transform things that are possible into things that are probable and things that are difficult into things that are easy. Through the presence of elegance we also transform the specter of chaos into the beauty of perfect order. Everything works better with elegance. In the coming chapters on the inner drivers and outer qualities, we will highlight the importance of continuous improvement and continuous development in a manner that promotes your pursuit of excellence. Your drivers and qualities represent the realities of who you already are, while continuous improvement promotes the dreams of who you aspire to be. Your pursuit of continuous improvement and continuous development helps you to pursue excellence in all of your endeavors. As joyous and uplifting as the pursuit of excellence can be, this chosen pursuit is not without its challenges. And while the mission of CIBIC is outwardly noble, the implementation of the CIBIC system will likely present you with a unique set of challenges that you must face and reconcile. Admiral Hyman G. Rickover was once quoted as saying "The devil is in the details, but so is salvation." Although some attempt to make continuous improvement a superficial pursuit, in its true sense, it is anything but superficial.

The truth of the matter is, the details that we may sometimes seek to discount can sometimes fuel our forward pursuits. With this in mind, we can now explore the inner drivers in comprehensive detail.

The Devil Is in the Details but So Is Salvation

HYMAN G. RICKOVER

Planning without Action Is Just as Bad as Action without Planning.

F. ALLEN DAVIS

3

Understanding the Inner Drivers

How can you be outwardly strong if you are inwardly weak? That question dominates the realm of continuous improvement. While some view excellence as a superficial pursuit, that view is flawed at best. In its truest sense, true excellence radiates from within, the manifestation of your inner strengths. Your inner dimension, inner persona, and inner attributes all fuel these inner strengths. By embracing this inner–outer connection, we promote the very balance that can drive our pursuit of excellence. While many factors influence this pursuit, no factor looms larger than the power of the mind as the primary promoter of change. In the realm of human existence, there is no power greater than the power of the mind. Your mind controls your thoughts, your thoughts control your actions, and your actions promote your pursuit of a better tomorrow. Those who embrace CIBIC learn that the systematic progression from inner power to outer strength is the fundamental driver of continuous improvement and the pursuit of excellence. As such, only the tireless and comprehensive development of your inner drivers can promote your pursuit of continuous improvement and excellence. Just like hydrogen powers the sun, your inner drivers power your mind, your soul, and your chosen pursuits. By recognizing, comprehending, and developing your inner drivers, you promote the pursuit of excellence at a wider scale, thus promoting the greater common good. This pursuit of excellence begins with your recognition of the inner drivers and their specific origins. The nine inner drivers and their refining subfactors highlight the attributes that promote your inner development. The nine inner drivers are stability, adaptability, planning, patience, humility, intelligence, resilience, enthusiasm, and sustainability. These nine inner drivers, which form the acronym SAPPHIRES, should be cherished like a prized possession. While traditionalists look for stars, CIBIC advocates seek out SAPPHIRES. By seeking out those who embrace the nine inner drivers, CIBIC practitioners and CIBIC enthusiasts highlight the collective values and skill sets that promote the pursuit of excellence from mediocrity. But before you can embrace the nine inner drivers, you must first understand their specific origins. The first driver of stability relates to your ability to create harmony across and throughout the wide-scope continuum. The second driver of adaptability relates to your inner endeavors to survive, thrive, adjust, respond, and sometimes conform in response to your adaptive and interactive challenges. The third driver of planning relates to your inner endeavors to cognitively plot your future course, approach, and direction. The fourth driver of patience relates to your inner ability to pause, wait, endure, anticipate, and otherwise cope with the time-based realities of life and your existence. The fifth driver of humility relates to your inner ability to embrace your humanity, spirituality, and decency. The sixth driver of intelligence relates to your inner ability to cognitively understand the world and all of its nuances. The seventh driver of resilience relates to your inner ability to persevere, withstand, and otherwise bounce back from adversity and setbacks. The eighth driver of enthusiasm relates to your inner ability to create, sustain, magnify, and otherwise perpetuate your mental and physical power and strength. And finally, the ninth driver of sustainability relates to your inner endeavors to embrace and promote safety, security, reliability, and quality as the essential promoters of continuity and perpetuity. These nine drivers form the essence of the inner dimensional DNA that controls your life and controls your world. And although your outer qualities may influence your relevance, these inner drivers drive your existence. With all of our potential, all of our abilities, and all of our gifts, we still exist by the grace of the maker, born with the potential to achieve great things. We are each unique among others, gifted in different ways, and capable of achieving what only we can achieve. And while the lazy, the apathetic, the callous, the entitled, and the amazingly fortunate may choose to discount the importance of drivers and qualities, the truly insightful and improvement driven among us recognize the role that these drivers and qualities play in the pursuit of excellence. Just like catalysts drive change, the inner drivers promote the infinite inner power and infinite potential that lies within. By embracing that power, we promote health, facilitate wealth, and enable the pursuit of happiness. While the nine inner drivers hold great importance, the 36 subfactors hold equal importance. The 36 subfactors highlight the four critical attributes or process elements of each inner driver. While inner drivers highlight wider critical attributes, the subfactors highlight very specific refined elements.

For stability, the four subfactors are uniformity, continuity, volatility, and demand. For adaptability, the four subfactors are interactive, functional, biological, and technical adaptability. For planning, the four subfactors are mission, objectives, strategy, and tactics. For patience, the four subfactors are intent, structure, progress, and temperament. For humility, the four subfactors are dignity, morality, decency, and philanthropy. For intelligence, the four subfactors are exposure, retention, application, and creation. For resilience, the four subfactors are vision, discipline, determination, and reinforcement. For enthusiasm, the four subfactors are physiology, psychology, motivation, and gratification. And for sustainability, the four subfactors are safety, security, reliability, and quality. These nine inner drivers and the 36 subfactors are highlighted in Figure 3.1. Just like elements combine to form compounds, the subfactors combine to comprise the foundation of the nine inner drivers. As you build an appreciation of each subfactor, your comprehension of continuous improvement should come into focus.

Consider the driver of stability, for example. In CIBIC, the pursuit of continuous improvement through stability is impossible without an understanding of the uniformity, continuity, volatility, and demand subfactors. The same rule applies to the other eight inner drivers. By extending the pursuit of continuous improvement into the subfactor realm, CIBIC adds a level of precision to your improvement endeavors, thus promoting the pursuit of excellence in a new and more imaginative way. This added precision helps to promote the effectiveness of the inner driver assessment tools that we will highlight later. By linking inner driver strength to subfactor prevalence, CIBIC elevates the pursuit of excellence, making it a much easier endeavor to comprehend and manage. Through this endeavor, we promote the elimination of gaps and chaotic realities in a manner that is both controllable and efficient. And as you will learn in later chapters, this control and efficiency also promotes the strength of your outer qualities. No matter who you are, where you live, and what your realities are, the inner drivers and outer qualities rule your world. With this narrative now complete, we can now delve into each of the nine inner drivers.

How Can You Be Outwardly Capable If You're Not Inwardly Functional?

F. ALLEN DAVIS

Appearances Are Often Deceiving.

AESOP

| Inner drivers |
| (SAPPHIRES) |

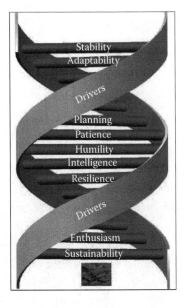

Stability
- Uniformity
- Continuity
- Volatility
- Demand

Adaptability
- Interactive
- Functional
- Biological
- Technical

Planning
- Mission
- Objectives
- Strategies
- Tactics

Patience
- Intent
- Structure
- Progress
- Temperament

Humility
- Dignity
- Morality
- Decency
- Philanthropy

Intelligence
- Exposure
- Retention
- Application
- Creation

Resilience
- Vision
- Discipline
- Determination
- Reinforcement

Enthusiasm
- Physiology
- Psychology
- Motivation
- Gratification

Sustainability
- Safety
- Security
- Reliability
- Quality

FIGURE 3.1
Your inner DNA—inner drivers and subfactors.

STABILITY

Stability is the first of the nine inner drivers that affect your success and your pursuit of excellence. In CIBIC, stability relates to your ability to create the near-term harmony that promotes your longer-term sustainability. Stability promotes that sustainability by efficiently regulating your near-term activities to promote your longer-term best interests. CIBIC promotes this pursuit by highlighting the importance of uniformity, continuity, volatility, and demand as stability influencing factors. By promoting rhyme, reason, and harmony, our stability helps us create order out of chaos, synergy out of discord, and unity out of conflict. While the active presence of stability is beneficial, the absence of stability can be cataclysmic. The absence of stability almost always promotes the gaps and chaotic realities that we would prefer to minimize, avoid, and prevent. Be it natural or artificial, limited or systemic, **static or dynamic**, or individual or collective, stability can manifest itself in many ways. Regardless of its origin, stability makes us stronger, more adaptable, and more resilient. While stability is often a state of mind, it can also be a state of presence or state of being. When stability is considered a state of mind, our inner endeavors become more critical. On the contrary, when stability is considered a state of presence or state of being, our outer endeavors become more critical. While some choose to disregard the importance of stability, that decision can promote significant consequences. The dynamic nature of our world and the unpredictable nature of human interactions make the pursuit of stability a perpetually challenging endeavor. Further magnifying this challenge is the relative nature of our views and perspectives. In the modern world, what may be stability promoting for some may be stability depleting for others. For this reason, the pursuit of stability must be a carefully planned and orchestrated endeavor. By recognizing and embracing the four subfactors of stability, the pursuit of stability becomes a much easier endeavor. At its foundation, as we discussed earlier, stability is the manifestation of four subfactors: **uniformity**, **continuity**, **volatility**, and **demand**. While your stability can be influenced in many ways, these subfactors typically have greater prominence. Your recognition of each of the four subfactors, beginning with uniformity, can truly influence your forward pursuits.

Uniformity

Uniformity is the first of the four stability subfactors. Uniformity in the realm of continuous improvement is only possible in the presence of the structure and standards that promote its existence. It is only through this structure and standardization that we create the static reality that promotes the pursuit of excellence and continuous improvement. Uniformity is the state or process of extending common core values, standards, and principles to a much wider demographic or frame of reference, reinforcing the importance of lateral consistency in the pursuit of excellence. By promoting structure and standardization, uniformity helps to create the structural integrity that almost always promotes quality and sustainability. While some diverse interests disregard the importance of uniformity, that decision can have far-reaching consequences. In the absence of uniformity, gaps and chaotic realities can reign supreme, causing great havoc. And while individuality and creativity are truly cherished values, there is a time and a place to embrace these values. When individuality and creativity corrupt the pursuit of excellence and sustainability, their value will always be diminished, individually and collectively. As a promoter of stability, uniformity is about the creation of common core values and common shared interests that, if continued ad infinitum, can promote our chosen pursuits. Uniformity highlights the common core values and common shared interests, at a **given static moment in time**, that promote the pursuit of excellence and sustainability. These common core values and common shared interests are usually highlighted and detailed in precisely structured activity, conformance, foundation, master, and strategic plans. While uniformity is about the creation of common core values and common shared interests, continuity is about the extension of these values and interests into a longer-term dynamic pursuit.

Continuity

Continuity is the second of the four stability subfactors. Be it to promote constant presence, constant performance, or constant progress, the importance of continuity is undeniable. Continuity represents our ability to promote, continue, or perpetuate a chosen dynamic pursuit over an extended period of time. By perpetuating the pursuit of excellence through our continuity, we help to promote an optimal reality for ourselves and others. While the presence of continuity can promote our pursuits, the absence of continuity can often be catastrophic. In the presence of bottlenecks, gridlock, stagnation, turbulence, and structural deficiencies, the pursuit of excellence can quickly become the pursuit of failure or mediocrity. Regardless of how these antagonists manifest themselves, it is ultimately your responsibility to prevent their existence before their existence becomes problematic. This prevention is only possible through your enthusiastic pursuit of the efficiency, good control, and good design that promotes perpetuity and excellence. At its foundation, however, the pursuit of continuity is heavily dependent on your ability and willingness to extend the scope of your planning endeavors into the pursuit of process standardization. Process standardization is the practice of using process diagrams and process diagnostics to improve the efficiency of work flows, process flows, and activity flows. Commonly used process diagram and process diagnostic tools include Gantt charts, PERT charts, and Ishikawa diagrams. PERT charts are graphical project management tools that are used to sequence activities and events within a given project, program, or endeavor. PERT, which is an acronym for Program Evaluation and Review Technique, was developed in the 1950s by the United States Navy to manage their submarine missile program. Gantt charts, on the other hand, are more detailed, itemized project management tools that are used to highlight the sequential activities and events within a given project, program, or endeavor. Gantt charts were originally created by Henry Gantt, an American mechanical engineer and management consultant. A third but nonetheless heavily used project management tool is the Ishikawa diagram, also referred to as the fishbone diagram. Ishikawa diagrams are cause-and-effect diagnostic tools that identify bottlenecks, gridlock, stagnation, turbulence, and structural deficiencies. The Ishikawa diagram was named after Kaoru Ishikawa, the modern father of cause-and-effect diagramming. When used properly, these process tools can help to create stability by creating the continuity and laminar flow that promotes that pursuit.

Volatility

Volatility is the third of the four stability subfactors. Volatility highlights the role that reactivity and response play in the pursuit of stability. Individuals, groups, and collective interests with higher levels of reactivity and volatility tend to react and respond to changing dynamics in more irrational and unpredictable ways, thus threatening the very stability that we wish to create and promote. As directly alluded to by Sir Isaac Newton, for every action, there is always some sort of reaction, sometimes equal and opposite. Even the economic world is influenced by this volatility. Economist Alfred Marshall illustrated the dynamics of volatility in the realm of economics through his supply-and-demand–driven principles of economics. No matter who you are, where you live, and what you do, volatility will always influence your chosen pursuits. While continuity is a manifestation of forward motion and uniformity is a manifestation of balance, volatility is a manifestation of your reaction to changes in motion and balance. In most situations, however, volatility is the manifestation of the surplus and deficit dynamics that are elements of demand.

Demand

Demand is the final of the four stability subfactors. Demand highlights the role that consumption and need play in the pursuit of stability. For individuals, groups, and collective interests, the significance of demand is undeniable and ever present. In the presence of greater or diminished demand for our services, products, bandwidth, time, and performance, our level of stability can vary, sometimes significantly. And while anticipation, forecasting, scalability, outsourcing, delegation, and contingency planning can help to dampen our demand-driven instabilities, they generally cannot eradicate these instabilities in their entirety. When consumption or need exceeds capacity, stress and other instabilities can emerge, sometimes with negative consequences. These instabilities, singularly or in tandem with volatility, can promote the very chaos that we are committed to avoid. While eradicating instabilities can aid your pursuits, only the enthusiastic pursuit of stability can guarantee that pursuit. And while the pursuit of stability can promote your best interests, it is only through the perpetuation of stability that we can truly promote the pursuit of excellence and continuous improvement. While this pursuit may seem easy to some, the ever-changing dynamics of demand make the pursuit of stability a uniquely challenging endeavor. Realities that used to change over decades in the past now change in months, introducing new instabilities to what was already a choppy and erratic endeavor. In the final analysis, only your ability to interpret and recognize these new realities will promote the pursuit of the stability you seek. Those who respond to these new realities will face a future of hope and promise, while those who can't will face a future of impending oblivion. With our stability narrative now complete, we can delve into the dynamics of adaptability, the second inner driver.

Continuity Does Not Rule Out Fresh Approaches to Fresh Situations.

DEAN RUSK

Ability Will Never Catch Up with the Demand for It.

CONFUCIUS

ADAPTABILITY

If stability promotes life and liberty, then adaptability promotes the pursuit of happiness. If you can't adapt, you can't sustain; if you can't sustain, you can't improve; and if you can't improve, achieving excellence becomes a virtual impossibility. Your reality and your certainty are if you can't adapt, you will always teeter on the cusp of oblivion and uncertainty. If the pursuit of adaptability, versatility, and flexibility is your goal, then your challenge, plain and simple, is to make adaptability your strength and not your weakness. Your transition to true adaptability is not without its challenges. We all view the world through different lenses, some clear, some clouded, and some tainted. Sometimes these lenses promote an open mind and sometimes they perpetuate a closed one. Regardless of your specific circumstances, becoming more adaptive will require you to master the **interactive**, **functional**, **biological**, and **technical** nuances of adaptability with all of their intricacies. While this pursuit may seem happenstance to some, learning the dynamics of adaptability is anything but easy. Since the beginning of time, the nuances of adaptability have confounded and mystified the masses. While interactive adaptability should be easy to pursue, promote, and sustain, our biases have made this pursuit anything but easy. Since the beginning of time, differences, distinctions, and variations that should be celebrated and embraced have become the crux of our divisions and our conflicts, turning what should be a perfect world into a not so perfect one. And despite our best attempts to promote diversity, inclusion, and reconciliation, society in general has still nonetheless struggled with the nuances of embracing a colorblind society. While some believe that interactive adaptability is our singular and predominant adaptability issue, nothing could be further from the truth. Even those who have conquered the nuances of interactive adaptability still face the wrath of functional, biological, and technical adaptability. With the ever-increasing nature of change in our modern society, mastering the nuances of functional adaptability has become an increasingly challenging endeavor. Every passing day brings new challenges, making the pursuit of functional adaptability a perpetually changing endeavor. Previous functional standards that may have promoted success in years gone by no longer yield the same result. And while the glory days of long ago may rekindle happy memories, the same standards of long ago have increasingly withered into obsolescence. While the elderly, historically disenfranchised, and other diverse interests have pointed the finger of blame in different directions, fewer causes loom larger than the nuances of technical adaptability. The dawn of the silicon age ushered in an overwhelming array of new technologies that, on one hand, made society more efficient and, on the other hand, made many diverse interests technically incapable and irrelevant. For these interests, technical innovation has created an array of adaptability challenges that are difficult and sometimes impossible to address and resolve. While interactive, functional, and technical adaptability are within our power to address through natural means, the final type of adaptability, biological adaptability, is much more difficult to address naturally. Inhabitable climates, spaces, depths, heights, and contaminated regions create biological antagonists that can be harmful or fatal. And while new technologies can address these antagonists, these technologies tend to be time limited and partial. The artificial habitats that we have ingeniously developed only promote our limited adaptability and short-term sustainability. Although the nuances of adaptability can challenge our resolve, we must still be willing to face these challenges with enthusiasm and vigor. While your superficial understanding of adaptability will aid you in that pursuit, only the comprehensive understanding of adaptability will expedite that pursuit. By first recognizing and acknowledging the great profound importance of adaptability, we help to promote the urgency of action that promotes the pursuit of excellence in this endeavor. By further recognizing the relevance of each of the four adaptability subfactors, we promote a greater understanding of their ability to promote, compromise, or limit the pursuit of adaptability. Your greater understanding of these subfactors begins with a thorough consideration of the interactive adaptability subfactor.

Interactive Adaptability

No adaptability element looms larger than interactive adaptability. Your ability and your willingness to recognize and embrace both quality and versatility in your interactive endeavors will undoubtedly influence your pursuit of excellence. While the shortsighted and the insecure shun the merits of adaptability, the truly insightful among us learn that only mutual respect and understanding, individually and collectively, can promote a better tomorrow. Your interactive versatility is the manifestation of your singular or collective propensity to embrace and successfully interact with the different gender, ethnic, religious, social, economic, and physical/mental disposition groups that exist in the modern world. Your interactive quality, on the other hand, represents the typical grade, caliber, character, and general traits possessed by individuals in your collaborative circle including your family, friends, peers, acquaintances, leaders, associations, and the media. Although the masses have historically struggled with the nuances of interactive adaptability, those who succeed in their chosen endeavors learn to embrace interactive adaptability as an essential precursor of excellence and continuous improvement. This pursuit must first and foremost be based on an uncompromising willingness to celebrate and not shun the individual and collective differences that exist in society, discounting the temptation to gravitate toward only those people who look, speak, and behave exactly as we do, shunning the temptation to be ethnocentric and ethnically biased. Within this endeavor, you must also be willing to **truthfully** acknowledge the positive and negative dynamics of each influence circle, avoiding the temptation to prematurely reach inaccurate and biased conclusions based on limited insight and limited exposure. In the interactive world, there are simply no absolutes. I often coin the phrase that ignorance does not discriminate. Translated, this phrase means that there is good and bad in every interactive group. However, within this reality, you must also be careful to acknowledge the interactive realities that exist in your influence circle. CIBIC promotes this pursuit by highlighting the four interactive quality categories that can be used to qualify your individual and collective interactions. These categories include the destroyer, contaminator, facilitator, and promoter categories. **Destroyers** are the masters of disaster and harbingers of pain who use coercion, persuasion, or outright hijacking to recruit and systematically destroy their victims. Their ability to hijack others is more formidable than most would ever imagine, and the instantaneous or delayed damage that they cause is a constant source of pain and discomfort for those that they manipulate. These are the people who cheat, steal, abuse, and otherwise promote criminal, unethical, or reckless activities. They are like a virus looking to replicate or destroy. They are the architects of their own demise and they can be the architect of your demise too if you allow it. **Contaminators** promote vulnerability and sometimes open the gateway for Destroyer influence. Although some choose to nonchalantly discount their influence, the reality is that Contaminators promote the behaviors, practices, values, and habits that will almost always lead to their self-destruction and yours if you allow it. Truancy, loitering, alcohol abuse, drug abuse, and seemingly harmless criminal mischief are just some of the dangers that Contaminators promote. Even limited exposure to Contaminators can create difficult circumstances down the line. In terms of Destroyers and Contaminators, Benjamin Franklin's quote that "an ounce of prevention is always better than a pound of cure" is truly worth careful consideration. Now that we have covered the two most dangerous influence categories, we can now discuss the two most favorable categories; Facilitators and Promoters. **Facilitators** are those with good intentions who can point you in the right direction and support your pursuit of a better tomorrow. Although they may not provide the material, professional, or intellectual support that you seek, they are still a gift that should be cherished and respected. Although Facilitators are truly a gift to be cherished, the Promoters are a gift to be embraced. **Promoters** are the beacons of hope who have the power, insight, resources, connections, and good intentions to power your pursuit of a better tomorrow. Otherwise referred to as your mentors, advisors, confidants, and moral leaders, these individuals and collective interest are what you need to succeed. If you are lucky enough to have Facilitators and Promoters in your midst, consider yourself lucky and learn what you can from each one of them. Once you embrace the pursuit of interactive versatility and successfully assess the interactive quality of your influence circle or circles, you will be better able to achieve excellence in your adaptability endeavors.

Functional Adaptability

Your functional adaptability includes your skill, concept, procedural, standard, and role-driven capabilities as influenced by your work ethic, values, principles, and preferences. Every life-specific, educational, career, professional, and task-specific endeavor has a corresponding set of functional expectations that are used to gauge your adaptability or lack thereof. Your specific level of adaptability is gauged by your mastery, competence, comprehension, or incompetence in each of your functional expectation categories. These category-specific expectations vary wildly based on the specific endeavor of emphasis. In some instances, functional mastery may be as simple as being able to add and subtract, while in other instances, it may be as complex as being able to precisely repair an artery. Ironically, what may exhibit basic competency in one functional category may exhibit mastery in another. The challenge for you is working to determine these expectations and dedicating yourself to the pursuit of mastery in your chosen endeavors. Although your skill, concept, procedural, standard, and role capabilities are the most predominant precursors of functional adaptability, physical health, stamina, good vision, and listening skills may also be equally important depending on your specific circumstances. As was the case with interactive adaptability, in functional adaptability, it is important for you to comprehend the four gauging qualifiers. Incompetence equates to your individual or collective inability to comprehend the nuances of a functional area. Comprehension equates to your individual or collective ability to comprehend and understand a functional area. Competency equates to your individual or collective ability to competently perform in a general functional area. And the final category, Mastery, equates to your individual or collective ability to perform at a very high level in a functional area. Even if you are able to conquer interactive and functional adaptability, two additional types of adaptability still remain; biological and technical adaptability.

Biological Adaptability

The ability to survive, endure, manage, or thrive in your environmental conditions is also a key determinant of your overall level of adaptability. Life in every life setting, neighborhood, city, county, state, country, continent, region, and ecosphere brings with it a unique set of biological challenges, some acute and some significant, that affect your survivability and your ability to adapt. From air, climate, and altitude considerations, to food, water quality, and environmental hazard prevalence, these biological and environmental considerations can affect your overall ability to adapt and survive. Some environments promote a sustainable natural existence, while other environments permit only an artificial existence. However, in the grander scheme, it is your specific ability to adapt to these varying biological circumstances that determines your actual level of biological adaptability. The specific varieties of biological incompatibilities are beyond comprehension to most people. Allergies, altitude susceptibility, and seasonal light disorders are just a few of this endless array of natural adaptability antagonists that can plague our natural existence. When you consider the equally lengthy list of man-made antagonists, it should be easier for you to see why this form of adaptability can wreak such widespread havoc. As was the case with the other subfactors, biological adaptability should always be gauged and measured using the four gauging qualifiers: survive, endure, manage, and thrive. The Survive category describes circumstances under which you or your collective interest have a basic ability to survive or minimally exist in a given environment.

The Endure category describes circumstances under which you or your collective interest have the ability to carve out a sustainable existence in a given environment. The Manage category describes circumstances under which you or your collective interest possess the ability to comfortably sustain and manage a long-term existence in a given environment. And the fourth category, Thrive, describes circumstances under which you or your collective interest are able to perform at a very high level. Even if you rate highly in the other three adaptability dynamics, one challenge still remains; the pursuit of technical adaptability.

Technical Adaptability

Your ability to adapt to the use of new products, new tools, new software, new communication devices, and new modern-day technologies is the fourth, but certainly not the least, important determinant of your overall adaptability. A close cousin of functional adaptability, technical adaptability gauges your ability to apply, create, use, and comprehend newly emerging and modern-day technologies, tools, and equipment. The rapid emergence of new technologies has greatly contributed to the increasing prevalence of this form of adaptability. While once considered an afterthought, technical adaptability has now risen to the critical necessity category. While competency in this category used to be classified as "geek" status, in modern times, it has become a general determinant of minimum competency. In recent years, the technical adaptability classification has shifted from the gauging of competency in using tools and equipment to competency in using required gadgets, contraptions, and systems. This usability shift has also ushered in an era of functional convergence and increasingly rapid product development. For the young, this rapidly changing technical landscape is "business as usual," but for the elderly, this rapidly changing technical landscape has created a never-ending series of challenges just to keep up, often resulting in an increasing number of people who get left behind in the wake of rapid innovation. As was the case with the other forms of adaptability that we discussed earlier, four gauging qualifiers highlight your ability to use new products, tools, software, and devices. In technical adaptability, the four gauging qualifiers are exposure, comprehension, competency, and mastery. The Exposure category equates to scenarios in which you or your collective interest have been generally exposed to a technical discipline or subject matter. The Comprehension category equates to scenarios in which you or your collective interest possess the ability to comprehend and understand a technical discipline or subject matter. The Competency category equates to scenarios in which you or your collective interest possess general competencies in a general technical discipline or subject matter. The fourth and final classifier, Mastery, equates to scenarios in which you or your collective interest possess a very high level of mastery in a technical discipline or subject matter. With our narrative of adaptability now complete, we can delve into the planning subject matter.

Adaptability Is Not Imitation.
It Means Power of
Resistance and Assimilation.

MAHATMA GHANDI

When You Make the World
Tolerable for Yourself, You
Make the World Tolerable
for Others.

VICTOR HUGO

PLANNING

In the realm of continuous improvement, planning is not only critical, it is essential. Your ability to pursue, achieve, and sustain excellence all rise from your ability to plan, develop, and formulate your forward pursuits. And while napkin planning may suffice for some, there is simply no substitute for down to the foundation "block and tackle" mission, objective, strategy, and tactical planning. Regardless of your specific circumstances, your pursuit of planning excellence begins with an understanding of what planning is, and what it isn't. Planning is not a short-term endeavor, and planning is not a passing fad. Planning is not about blind faith and knee jerk reactions. Planning is acknowledging the realities of who you are, and embracing the vision of who you desire to be. It is only through the endeavor of planning that your dreams and ambitions can truly become your realities. While far too many discount the endeavor of planning, the truly insightful among us learn that successful planning requires a clear vision, tireless commitment, and perpetual consistency. Although the perceived importance of planning can vary from person to person and group to group, make no mistake that planning is, and will always be, critically important to us all. Planning promotes survival for some, safety for others, and prosperity for everyone else. Despite its power, planning remains a sadly underpracticed and underutilized endeavor. For far too many, the lack of commitment and discipline dooms their planning endeavors before they begin. While many individuals, groups, and collective interests succeed at initial plan development, most fail at the full and tireless implementation of those plans as crafted. Conflicting priorities, time constraints, lack of commitment, and lack of discipline often undermine the successful implementation of these plans, leading to poor performance and the lack of planned progress. These confounding circumstances result in the 20% successful implementation rate that plagues most individuals, groups, and collective interests. Simply recognizing these confounding circumstances can significantly promote the successful implementation of these plans as written. But first and foremost, planning is about the creation of a path forward from your current realities to your desired realities. By bridging the gap between your wants and needs and your current realities, the endeavor of planning helps to promote your hopes, dreams, and an optimal existence. While some view planning as a narrow pursuit, it is anything but narrow. Planning is the manifestation of four key elements: mission, objective, strategy, and tactical elements. Described hereafter using the MOST (**M**ission, **O**bjectives, **S**trategies, and **T**actics) acronym, these four key elements promote the success of your planning endeavors. Your **mission** development involves successfully crafting your reason or reasons for existing in very finite and refined terms. Your **objective** development involves the active and substantive recognition and identification of evaluating analytics or metrics that gauge your progress against a set of mission-promoting goals. Your **strategy** development involves the active and substantive recognition and identification of goal-promoting methods and dynamics that uniquely articulate your planned approach for achieving a mission and objective. And, your **tactic** development highlights the very specific actions that support your chosen strategy. Together, these four planning elements describe and promote the endeavor of planning in its entirety. For those who embrace the fundamental, comprehensive, and continual use of planning, the future holds infinite potential and infinite possibilities. For those who shun, discount, or otherwise disregard the importance of planning, life, liberty, and the pursuit of happiness will always hang in the balance. Although a superficial understanding of the mission, objective, strategy, and tactical elements of planning will promote your success, only a comprehensive review of this subject matter will truly promote your pursuit of excellence and continuous improvement. Understanding the dynamics of mission development is a critical first step.

Mission

In the endeavor of planning, your mission determination is necessary, essential, and critical. Your mission captures the dynamics of who or what you currently are, and who or what you desire to be in fully descriptive detail. Your mission captures your reason or reasons for existing, and the planned impact that you desire to have in your individual, group, and collective endeavors. Although your mission dynamics can vary greatly based on your timing, scope, and scale, the minimal inclusions are generally constant. Your mission dynamics should include both the internal and external considerations that help to promote balance and transparency. Your mission dynamics should also include at least one element that addresses the prevailing gaps and chaotic realities that exist. While single element mission statements continue to be embraced, in CIBIC, a multiple element mission structure is promoted. This multiple element mission structure supports the efficient and well-structured selection of objectives, strategies, and tactics that will truly promote your pursuit of excellence and sustainability. The importance of careful mission statement craftsmanship will become apparent when you consider the intricacies of objectives determination. In terms of gauging metrics, your strength or weakness in this subfactor is indicated using one of four descriptors: nonexistent progress, minimal progress, substantial progress, or significant progress. The dynamics of this descriptor will be highlighted further in the inner driver metrics section.

Objectives (Goals)

While mission determination is critically important, the next endeavor in planning is no less important. If your mission is your ultimate destination, then your objectives are the specific milestones and markers for reaching that destination. While objective determination has been practiced since the beginning of time, our management of this endeavor has changed markedly in modern times. Objective determination is the practice or endeavor of identifying the actionable elements that resolve or otherwise eliminate your mission-specific gaps. When you quantify and qualify these gaps as part of the objective determination process, you create the potential for continuous improvement. This process also gives rise to the use of metrics and analytics as improvement-promoting tools. While the use of metrics and analytics used to be considered a "geekish" fad, in modern times, the use of metrics and analytics has become an expected, essential, and mandatory practice. The prevalence of metrics and analytics has increased so markedly that they have now become the cornerstones of modern business management and performance determination. By combining the objective determination and analytics endeavors, you make the pursuit of excellence and continuous improvement a much easier endeavor to promote and sustain. When you further incorporate the EDGE framework configuration, development, deployment, and continuation progressions into this process, your planning integrity should improve markedly. By additionally incorporating three to five objective elements for each mission element, you further strengthen your planning endeavor, adding new detail and competencies into what has been generally a hit-and-miss endeavor for most interests. The inclusion of this new detail also promotes the enhanced use of metrics and analytics as a success-promoting tool, further expanding the scope of performance measurement. As is the case with the other subfactors, the selection of gauging factors is critically important. In objective determination, your level of progress or lack thereof is highlighted using one of four descriptors: nonexistent progress, minimal progress, substantial progress, or significant progress. This descriptor will also be further highlighted in the inner driver metrics section.

Strategy

Once you have crafted your mission, identified your gaps, and chosen your objectives, your next challenge is the selection of the strategy or strategies that will promote the pursuit of excellence through gap elimination. But what is strategy? Your strategy is the objectives-driven "game plan" for resolving, eliminating, or otherwise managing gaps and chaotic factors. Mathematician and chess master Max Euwe once stated that "Strategy requires thought, tactics require observation" while ancient Chinese war strategist Sun Tzu once stated that "all men can see these tactics whereby I conquer, but what none can see is the strategy out of which victory evolved." At a higher level, strategy is the cognitive approach for creating excellence out of mediocrity and failure. While your chosen strategies can promote your success, the development of those strategies is neither easy nor simple for the inexperienced. The dynamic nature of the world and the complex nature of our circumstances make strategy creation both tedious and challenging. While the masses tend to shun this endeavor, CIBIC practitioners and CIBIC enthusiasts learn to face this challenge with enthusiasm and a sense of purpose. They learn to view strategy development as a structured pursuit that is easy to master. While strategy creation is inherently complex, CIBIC makes this creation dramatically easier. In CIBIC, strategies are created by selecting eight strategy-specific attributes as highlighted in Figure 3.2. These attributes highlight the four goal attributes and four method attributes that promote the creation of an effective strategy. The four *goal* attributes highlight the goal qualifier, goal action, goal target, and goal outcome that describe the dynamics of what you are pursuing. The **goal qualifier** is an adverb that is used to refine and qualify the specific goal-driven action that is proposed. The **goal action** is a verb that highlights the specific goal-promoting action that will be used to achieve the desired result. The **goal target** attribute is a noun that highlights the specific party that will be the intended beneficiary target of the strategic action. The final goal attribute is the **goal outcome** attribute

Goal qualifier	Aggressively	Progressively	Proactively
	Reactively	Procedurally	Reducibly
	Producibly	Regressively	

Goal action	Accumulate	Defend	Facilitate
	Achieve	Disable	Improve
	Acquire	Discover	Preserve
	Attack	Develop	Promote
	Control	Empower	Protect
	Create	Enable	Pursue

Goal target	Client	Employer	Organizational
	Community	Family	Partner
	Competitor	Group	Peer
	Constituent	Individual	Rival
	Departmental	Institutional	Societal
	Divisional	National	World

Goal outcome	Approval	Interests	Safety
	Assessments	Performance	Stability
	Assets	Position	Standing
	Balance	Prosperity	Success
	Efficiency	Rating	Support
	Growth	Resources	Victory

Method speed	Careful	Orchestrated	Delayed
	Quantum	Incremental	Rapid
	Methodical	Slow	

Method approach	Creation	Exploitation	Development
	Investment	Disruption	Representation
	Engagement	Utilization	Misrepresentation

Method target	Client(s)	Employer(s)	National
	Community	Family	Natural
	Competitor(s)	Group(s)	Organizational
	Constituent(s)	Individual(s)	Partner(s)
	Departmental	Institutional	Peer(s)
	Divisional	Investor	Advocate(s)

Method emphasis	Attributes	Proximity	Economics
	Mentality	Image	Resources
	People	Skills	Goodwill

FIGURE 3.2

The key elements of strategy.

that highlights the specific end effect that is desired in general qualitative terms. The four *method* attributes highlight the method speed, method approach, method target, and method emphasis that qualify how you will pursue your desired goal. The **method speed** attribute is an adverb that highlights the timing dynamic of your chosen method approach. The **method approach** attribute is a verb that highlights the tangible leveraging dynamic that will be used in your strategic endeavors. The **method target** attribute is a noun that highlights the specific tangible target of your strategic endeavors. And finally, the **method emphasis** dynamic highlights the tangible or intangible economic, image, interpersonal, proximity, mentality, resource, and skill attributes among others. In strategy development, these eight strategy attributes are combined to form a strategy statement that highlights the specific strategy or strategies that will be used to achieve a specific goal. Although this simplified approach to strategy development may seem somewhat limiting, nothing could be further from the truth. The CIBIC strategy development approach supports the creation of more than 400 million (429,981,696) distinct strategy statements, an incredibly large number. Once you complete the development of your strategy or strategies, the selection of your tactics becomes a much easier endeavor.

In terms of gauging metrics, as is the case with the other subfactors, your strength or weakness in this subfactor is indicated using one of four descriptors: nonexistent progress, minimal progress, substantial progress, or significant progress. The dynamics of this descriptor will also be highlighted in the inner driver metrics section.

Tactics

Whereas strategies are the manifestation of your objectives, your tactics are the outward manifestation of your strategies and your strategic intent. Once you determine your mission, select your objectives, and craft your strategy, the selection of your tactics becomes a much simpler endeavor. Tactics drive your actions, drive your work, drive your operations, drive your programs, and drive your activities. In a perfect world, your strategy should represent the sum of your tactics, and your tactics should represent the sum of your actions. When you effectively develop your tactics, the ambiguities concerning the who, what, where, when, why, and how elements of planning should disappear entirely. While tactics and strategies are often confused as being the same thing, nothing could be further from the truth. Strategies promote tactical execution while tactics promote incremental progress. Strategies are driven by complex cognitive decisions while tactics are driven by specific required actions. In terms of gauging metrics, as is the case with the other subfactors, your strength or weakness in this subfactor is indicated using one of four descriptors: nonexistent progress, minimal progress, substantial progress, or significant progress. The dynamics of this descriptor will also be highlighted in the inner driver metrics section. With our planning narrative now complete, we can delve into the dynamics of patience, the fourth inner driver.

Plan Your Work and Work Your Plan.

VARIOUS UNKNOWN

If You Plan to Be Great, and Work to Be Great, Then Great You Shall Be.

F. ALLEN DAVIS

PATIENCE

While the nine inner drivers have collective importance, the importance of patience is uniquely distinct. Your maturity, professionalism, wisdom, and insight all rise from your ability and willingness to be patient. Patience highlights your ability to comprehend, withstand, tolerate, and otherwise cope with the time relevance and time sensitivities of your chosen endeavors. Your ability to be precise, detailed, mature, and refined all rise from your capacity to be patient. While many view patience as a cherished virtue, others view patience as a status quo promoter. While excessive patience may promote delay and the status quo, it also promotes the endurance and strength of character that leads to long-term progress. Be it on a large or small scale, patience almost always promotes the pursuit of excellence and continuous improvement, especially when it promotes inner driver development. Patience, as an inner driver, is the manifestation of four patience subfactors: **intent**, **structure**, **progress**, and **temperament**. Intent highlights the goals, objectives, and deliverables of your chosen pursuits. Before you can be patient, you must first have something to be patient about. Structure and compliance highlight the standards, rules, and regulations that apply to your chosen pursuits. While the undisciplined and impatient among us would prefer to live in a world free of structure, the reality is that most worthwhile endeavors have rules and regulations of one type or another. Progress highlights and indicates your level of advancement in the pursuit of a desired goal, objective, or deliverable. It is ultimately our perceived progress toward a stated goal that promotes or obstructs our level of patience. While our progress is important, our response to that progress can be just as important. Temperament highlights our emotional response to setbacks, obstructions, and disappointments. A close cousin of volatility, the lack of good temperament can promote emotional tirades and temper tantrums. While some view patience as constant and perpetual, nothing could be further from the truth. Our experiences, our relationships, our circumstances, and our culture can significantly affect the manifestation of patience. And while patience is truly an honorable virtue, it is ultimately your desire to be patient that promotes your level of success or lack thereof. Patience is a gift that is pursued by many and possessed by few. In the absence of patience, inconsiderate behavior, inadequate professionalism, and inordinate levels of instant gratification can often reign supreme. These three behavioral antagonists, singularly or collectively, can promote the perpetual dysfunctionality, disillusionment, and disappointment that have laid claim to far too many, promoting the gaps and chaotic realities that always loom in the distance. Only your willingness and desire to promote patience as a cherished value will mitigate the risk of disillusionment, disappointment, and disgust that disproportionately plagues far too many in the instant gratification era. As is the case with the other inner drivers, this willingness and desire begin with a more in-depth understanding of the four subfactors of patience, beginning with intent.

Intent

Intent is the first of the four patience subfactors. Although structure, progress, and temperament play a major role in the manifestation of patience, your intent or lack thereof can play an even greater role. At its foundation, intent describes the quantifiers and qualifiers of a chosen pursuit. In general terms, there are three types of intent: general intent, specific intent, and indirect intent. General intent highlights the general dynamics of your chosen pursuits in very broad terms. Specific intent highlights the very specific dynamics of your chosen pursuits in very narrow terms. Indirect intent highlights the unspecified and unstated dynamics of your chosen pursuits, dynamics that exist in fact for which you have not directly acted toward. Whether it be learning a skill, acquiring an asset, reaching a destination, or achieving a goal, the quantification and qualification of your chosen pursuits establish the intent dynamic of those pursuits. While recognizing your intent may appear to be easy, itemizing your intentions is generally anything but easy. Planning dynamics, interpersonal influences, cultural norms, and your collective experiences can each influence your specific intentions. Your challenge is to qualify and quantify your general, specific, and indirect intentions and use that insight to promote your pursuit of patience. By achieving excellence in the qualification and quantification of your intent, you help to promote greater levels of patience through greater comprehension and heightened awareness.

Structure

While intent highlights the focus of your chosen pursuits, structure highlights the standards, rules, and regulations that guide those pursuits. As we discussed earlier, structure and compliance highlight the standards, rules, and regulations that apply to your pursuits. We all live with structure of one form or another. While some structure regulates our efforts, other structure regulates the efforts of others. While structure that regulates your current activities will invariably delay your chosen pursuits, structure that regulates the efforts of others will invariably delay your collective progress due to no cause of your own. Our laws, our certification standards, our professional principles, and our minimum achievement standards are all forms of structure that can sometimes delay and regulate our pursuit of a chosen goal. While some structure can promote frustration, other structure can promote greater levels of patience by providing more time-based information about a chosen pursuit. It is ironic that in some situations, impatience can be the manifestation of the lack of information about a chosen endeavor, as opposed to the actual time realities of that endeavor. In countless instances and circumstances, structured endeavors that are well conceived and imaginatively structured can significantly promote higher levels of patience. From electronic applications that provide service availability detail to premium pay services that provide rapid access to service resources and capabilities, the use of structure to address patience continues to flourish. From amusement park fast passes and highway limited access lanes to restaurant reservation and limited waiting applications, these structured time management tools continue to gain greater and greater acceptance with consumers and service providers alike. But while many embrace these new solutions, many more embrace the older proven solutions. From tabloid placement to video entertainment, the old and proven solutions continue to be used. And be it in a grocery store or a vehicle service waiting area, these solutions continue to entertain and amuse, diverting attention from the wait being experienced.

Progress

As we discussed earlier, progress highlights the advancements made in the general pursuit of a goal, objective, or deliverable. When we experience traffic gridlock, poor performance, long restaurant waiting lines, and delayed gratification, a very natural disappointment stimulus arises. That stimulus forms the basis of our emotional response to the actual delay or lack of progress. As the level of progress increases and decreases, a range of emotions can ensue from temper tantrums and disillusionment to disappointment and disgust. When significant progress is made toward a goal, objective, or deliverable, the level of disappointment tends to be small. However, when limited progress is made toward a goal, objective, or deliverable, the level of disappointment tends to be much larger. Our exhibited level of patience is directly proportional to this level of disappointment. While the outward reaction to this disappointment can vary widely from person to person and from group to group, your volatility or lack thereof as exhibited by the prevailing temperament can significantly influence exhibited emotions.

Temperament

As we discussed earlier, temperament highlights our relative response to the level of progress or lack thereof. While your experiences and situations can sometimes influence your temperament, your culture and your close relationships tend to be much more impactful. And while your intent, structure, and progress can mitigate your exhibited temperament, these three subfactors can only modestly change the prevailing natural temperament that exists. While intent, structure, and progress tend to be more consistently measured, the measure of temperament can vary widely. While your prevailing temperament may be considered normal in your typical surroundings, that same temperament can and often will be assessed differently in different environments and surroundings. Further complicating your understanding of temperament is the very complex nature and nurture considerations. While nature applies on a grander scale and nurture applies on a smaller scale, the influence of each on the dynamics of temperament is unavoidable and undeniable. Our prevailing temperament can vary significantly based on our natural and environmental circumstances. While a long delay in grocery store checkouts may be reasonable and customary in one area, that same delay may be deemed totally unacceptable in a different area. These prevailing norms can often change our perception of what is typical and customary by altering our prevailing expectations. The expectations, when reinforced over an extended period, create natural tendencies that we often embrace indefinitely. Recognizing the role that temperament plays in the pursuit of patience can go a long way in promoting the successful progress that reinforces your pursuit of excellence. By recognizing the difference between calm and volatile temperaments in prevailing environments, we help to promote the pursuit of excellence through greater awareness and understanding. In the CIBIC system, when patience is expected, patience is embraced, and when patience is embraced, patience will prevail. By developing an in-depth understanding of the intent, structure, progress, and temperament subfactors of patience, we promote the level of patience that facilitates the pursuit of excellence and continuous improvement.

Genius Is Eternal Patience.

MICHAELANGELO

He That Can Have Patience Can Have What He Will.

BENJAMIN FRANKLIN

HUMILITY

While planning and patience are both essential to your pursuit of excellence, they pale in comparison to the importance of humility and its impact on humanity. Be it ever so humble, humility as an honorable virtue stands alone. Humility highlights your propensity to embrace dignity, morality, decency, and philanthropy as honorable virtues. While those who promote arrogance and mischief disrupt life, liberty, and the pursuit of happiness, those who embrace humility promote the pursuit of a better tomorrow through their actions and their values. While some view humility as a widely held virtue, that view has no basis in fact. The increasing prevalence of personal biases, corrupting influences, and run amok indecency has made the high prevalence of humility the exception, and sadly not the rule. However, for those with strength of character and strength of conviction, the pursuit of humility need not be an impossible dream. When humility thrives, we prevail, but when humility wanes, we falter, individually and collectively. While the presence of humility promotes a better world, the presence of its evil twin, arrogance and mischief, promotes a more destructive one. While ambition is generally a good thing, ambition laced with excessive arrogance and mischief is generally humility limiting and destructive. Like a pandemic run amok, arrogance and mischief give rise to indecency, immorality, and indignity, damaging our hopes for a better tomorrow. While some view this arrogance and mischief as funny, cool, trendy, and apropos, such a view is destructive at best. The great philosopher Confucius once said, "Humility is the solid foundation of all virtues," while philosopher and early Quaker William Penn once stated that "Humility and knowledge in poor clothes excel pride and ignorance in costly attire." While some believe humility, as a principle, is widely embraced and promoted by the well endowed, successful, and entitled, such a view is not always the case. Sadly, the pursuit of material gain can make otherwise responsible individuals and collective interests do unimaginably horrible things in pursuit of wealth, compromising their values for ill-begotten gain and failing to answer a perpetually looming question: what good is being rich, if it makes you poor? In a truly perfect world, humility should be practiced by all, and embraced by all. By rejecting indecency, immorality, and indignity, we preserve, protect, and defend our most cherished values. But when we embrace these same indecencies, immoralities, and indignities, we promote the catastrophes that always loom in the distance. Everywhere you look, these catastrophes are widely prevalent and never ending. From the Wall Street-inspired financial meltdown to the savings and loan travesty, the damaging effects of arrogance and mischief are ever menacing and ever present. And while the pursuit of affluence is often at the root of these damaging behaviors, the absence of affluence can be just as damaging. From gang-promoting and discriminatory behavior to terrorism and criminal mischief, the damaging effects of arrogance and mischief are troublesome and detrimental. While some discount arrogance and mischief as damaging manifestations, CIBIC practitioners and CIBIC enthusiasts learn to view both manifestations as equally troublesome and equally damaging. When we fail to recognize and acknowledge the damaging nature of arrogance and mischief, we promote the very biases that have already done far too much damage to the societal landscape. And while the seemingly meaningless absence of good manners and responsible conduct may be dismissed by some as insignificant, these harbingers of impending arrogance can often be the sign of looming trouble in the distance. Be it failing to say thank you, failing to hold open a door, using indecent language, embracing gang affiliation, embracing terrorist sympathies, or exhibiting gender and ethnic biases, these troublesome behaviors promote the early onset of much more serious problems. No matter how large or small, arrogance and mischief are damaging, damning, and detrimental to the pursuit of excellence and continuous improvement. Rather than focusing on arrogance and mischief as the antagonists of humility, CIBIC turns attention to the tendencies and behaviors that promote humility. These tendencies and behaviors are highlighted in the form of the four subfactors of humility: dignity, morality, decency, and philanthropy. By promoting high moral values and positive intent, the four subfactors of humility promote the pursuit of excellence and continuous improvement through positive action and positive intent. As was the case with the other inner drivers, your ability to promote humility begins and ends with a more in-depth understanding of the four subfactors of humility, beginning with dignity.

Dignity

Although many definitions exist for dignity, the most appropriate definition is the sense of pride and self-respect for oneself. Although dignity is a virtue that should be possessed by all, that is not always the case. The ever more prevalent number of arrogance and mischief promoting individual and collective interests continue to plague modern society and our collective best interests. From factions and gangs to fear mongers and demagogues, dignity-ravaging interests have driven the pursuit of dignity into the realm of the improbable. While personal pride and self-respect used to be widely embraced, that no longer seems to be the case. Be it from malaise or spite, this emerging general lack of dignity is both troublesome and destructive. And be it from a sense of worthlessness, truancy, immorality, insignificance, or ignominy, the lack of dignity makes the pursuit of excellence and continuous improvement improbable and sometimes impossible. While the culpable factions, gangs, fear mongers, and demagogues are partly to blame for this rapidly eroding dignity prevalence, no cause looms larger than our self-promoted lack of self-worth and self-respect. Although the lack of opportunity is sometimes to blame for higher indignity prevalence, that problem alone should never erode dignity in its entirety. There is simply no substitute for dignity, and no excuse for not embracing it with enthusiasm. After all, how can we expect other people to respect us if we don't first respect ourselves? If you have already embraced dignity and a dignified existence, then consider yourself fortunate, but if you lack dignity, then you should consider this question your wake-up call. Dignity is about building pride through self-respect and righteousness. Dignity is also about acknowledging the dynamics of who you are, and embracing the dream of who you aspire to be, individually and collectively. By embracing the dynamics of your future and your past, you promote dignity and greater self-appreciation. This greater level of dignity and self-appreciation will help you in your endeavors to find and pursue your path to a better tomorrow. Make no mistake, however; finding the right path and staying on that path are two separate endeavors. Once you find the right path, you must be willing to remain on that path, not letting the harbingers of failure distract you from your mission. You must be willing to embrace personal pride and self-respect as the promoters of a better tomorrow. Nelson Mandela once stated that "Any man or institution that tries to rob me of my dignity will lose." Although our basic survival instincts may be prevalence of dignity, we must nonetheless challenge ourselves to embrace the pursuit of dignity as a critical necessity.

Morality

While dignity is generally self-centric in focus, morality is generally all-inclusive in nature. Our morality promotes our ability to gauge right from wrong, ethical from unethical, fair from unfair, and good from bad in our societal endeavors. By helping us to gauge our actions from the wider societal points of view, morality promotes humility on a wider scale, accelerating our pursuit of a better tomorrow. Mahatma Gandhi once stated that "Morality is the basis of things, and truth is the substance of all morality," and French philosopher Albert Camous once stated that "A man without ethics is a wild beast let loose upon this world." Regardless of which definition you embrace, there is simply no substitute for the grand importance of morality. In CIBIC, morality is the manifestation of eight critical dynamics: restriction, reciprocity, origination, transparency, intent, viability, damage, and legality. Restriction relates to the tendency to coerce, inhibit, enslave, control, and otherwise limit freedom through forced action, demagoguery, or trickery. Reciprocity relates to the tendency to restrict, inhibit, or otherwise limit balance, equality, access, or fairness for reasons of personal gain or bias. Origination relates to the tendency to unfairly act or otherwise function based on reasons of unfair affiliation, unjustifiable personal biases, and undue cause. Transparency relates to the intent to promote clarity and clear interpretation to reveal the true facts or circumstances of a given situation. Intent relates to the tendency to properly consider the far-reaching impact of a specific end goal of a given action. Viability relates to the tendency to choose a legitimate and practical path forward that will be optimally valid in the long term while providing significant benefit to all involved parties. Damage relates to the tendency to contaminate, exterminate, assault, cleanse, and otherwise promote harm to others. And legality relates to the tendency to promote, support, conduct, fund, or influence activities that are deemed to be illegal. While some dynamics promote transparency, others promote fairness and decency. From the Foreign Corrupt Practices Act and the Ford–Dodd Act to the Sarbanes–Oxley Act, the pursuit of transparency, fairness, and decency in the public domain continues to have great importance. Coupled with the different individual, legal, legislative, regulatory, and commercial endeavors that promote morality, it is easy to understand why the pursuit of morality has such great importance. While some endeavors address financial misconduct and others address tyrannical, environmental, criminal, racial, and religious misconduct, each of these endeavors help to promote the collective best interest through preemptive action and aggressive prevention. Morality helps us to avoid the upheavals, strife, and conflict that if left unchecked can unravel the fabric of society in the near term and ad infinitum. When we embrace morality and its close cousin, decency, we help to promote a better tomorrow.

Decency

The pursuit of decency is an endeavor that continues to challenge our modern society in many ways, shapes, and forms. Although the right to creativity and self-expression is guaranteed in many democracies, the use and application of these rights continue to create behavioral and regulatory challenges that we continue to struggle with as a society. While public nudity may be viewed as a form of public self-expression for some, it is viewed as indecent by others, thus creating a source of perpetual disagreement. And while the right of free speech is also guaranteed in many democratic societies, that right, when pushed beyond reasonable boundaries, is also a source of spirited disagreement. In these and other instances, it is important for you to establish reasonable and customary standards for decency that are appropriate, legal, justifiable, and enforceable. Establishing and maintaining these standards will always present you with perpetual challenges. When these decency standards are overly biased, excessively infringing on the rights of others, then legal difficulties are sure to follow. When these standards, on the other hand, are designed to promote life, liberty, humility, and the pursuit of happiness, then the use and interpretation of these standards tends to be a much more thought-provoking endeavor. In general terms, decency is the manifestation of your conduct, appearance, or message as measured by the predetermined standards of morality and respectability. Conduct relates to your actions and the tendency of your actions to be viewed of as rude, insensitive, vulgar, disrespectful, inappropriate, or overly aggressive. Appearance relates to your visual presence and the tendency of your appearance to be viewed of as inappropriate, vulgar, or distasteful. Message relates to your visual and verbal interactions and the tendency of these interactions to be viewed of as lewd, distasteful, menacing, and generally inappropriate. Although some would argue that the measure of decency is always a constant standard, that is generally never the case. Behavior that is deemed decent in one scenario may not be viewed the same way in other scenarios. As such, in your decency-related interactions, your challenge is to first recognize what is relevant and acceptable and then acknowledge or respond to those realities accordingly. Your second challenge is to make sure that your choices do not detract from your pursuit of decency and humility in general terms. Although the lack of decency may be viewed by some as cool, fun, stylish, or even trendy, care must be taken to make sure that these views don't interfere with your pursuit of a better tomorrow. You must also be careful to recognize that your lack of willingness to be cool, fun, stylish, and trendy can sometimes promote unpleasant consequences, especially in areas where ignorance and achievement-driven naivete reign supreme. If this scenario relates to your specific circumstances, you should plan accordingly, acknowledging the realities that exist. But regardless of your specific circumstances, you must also be willing to embrace the pursuit of excellence as the fundamental driver of your future pursuits.

Philanthropy

While dignity, morality, and decency tend to be the inner building blocks of humility, philanthropy tends to be the outer manifestation of our humility. The dignified, moral, and decent among us tend to be philanthropic, while the philanthropic tend to be dignified, moral, and decent in all but extreme instances. Henry David Thoreau once stated that "Philanthropy is almost the only true virtue which is sufficiently appreciated by mankind." Some call philanthropy the eagerness and willingness to make the world a better place, others call it the enthusiasm to provide material support, and yet others call it the willingness to embrace fellowship with mankind. No matter the definition of philanthropy, the one certainty is that philanthropy helps to make the world a better place. When we volunteer for public or private service, we show an affinity to help mankind, and when we donate to charitable causes, we support a culture of giving back to society. Although volunteering, donating, and otherwise giving back are at the center of philanthropy, the joy of spiritual fellowship is not far behind. The pursuit of spiritual fellowship, no matter what type, is deeply woven into the fabric of modern society. Whether it be from the pulpit, minbar, tebah, altar, or living room, the glory of spirituality and its role in philanthropy should never be discounted. Regardless of your specific philanthropic tendencies, it is important for you to embrace and acknowledge the role that philanthropy plays in the pursuit of humility as an inner driver. As long as philanthropy is pursued and embraced in a manner that discounts self-serving bias and demagogic exploitation, then the pursuit will almost always be an admirable one. With our humility narrative now complete, we can delve into the very important subject matter of intelligence.

Power Tends to Corrupt,
Absolute Power Tends
to Corrupt Absolutely.

LORD JOHN DALBERG-ACTION

Humility and Knowledge in
Poor Clothes Excel Pride
and Ignorance in Costly
Attire.

WILLIAM PENN

INTELLIGENCE

The exposure to, retention of, application of, and creative use of intelligence are key determinants of an optimal existence. Stephen Hawking once stated that "Intelligence is the ability to adapt to change," and Albert Einstein once stated that "The true sign of intelligence is not knowledge but imagination." Unlike the other eight inner drivers, intelligence holds the distinction of being a highly complex dynamic. The complexity arises from the presence of its four standard subfactors and its nine distinctive functional types. The four intelligence subfactors of exposure, retention, application, and creation highlight the four ways that intelligence manifests itself, while the nine functional intelligence types are used to segment and qualify the nine types of intelligence. The nine intelligence types, which include core, basic, spatial, creative, naturalistic, mathematical, linguistic, interactive, and physiological intelligence, help us to classify and comprehend the unique forms of intelligence. **Core intelligence** is the intrapersonal, spiritual, and foundational form of intelligence that is the nature of our inner dimensional intelligence. Our religious beliefs, our values, our preferences, and our principles are all key elements of our core intelligence. **Basic intelligence** is the foundation from which our ability to apply, interpret, and analyze originates from. Our basic intelligence originates from our ability to acquire knowledge and information through active learning. The sum of your acquired knowledge and information is equal to your total basic intelligence. **Visual and spatial intelligence** is the ability to intelligently analyze, interpret, and manipulate visual or spatial information, shapes, forms, and details. Visual and spatial intelligence requires abstract thinking and applied reasoning capabilities. People with high levels of visual and spatial intelligence find comfort living in a realm full of "what if" questions and have the gift of being able to see things that others can't see. **Applied creative intelligence** is the ability to artistically create art, music, graphics, pictures, and sensory tantalizing works. People with high levels of applied creative intelligence live in the realm of creating works that attract and excite through sound, sight, smell, taste, and touch. **Naturalistic intelligence** is the ability to grow, nurture, recognize, appreciate, protect, and otherwise perpetuate nature in all of its majesty. Plants, flowers, species, air, water, earth, ecology, geology, geography, weather, the general environment, and the natural world are all in the realm of naturalists and those with naturalistic intelligence. **Applied mathematical**

intelligence is the ability to interpret, analyze, derive, apply, or otherwise manipulate mathematical data. People with high applied mathematical intelligence have a heightened ability to describe, predict, map, and otherwise understand the different mathematical patterns of nature. **Verbal and linguistic intelligence** is the ability to verbally communicate, accurately spell, creatively articulate, and otherwise verbally, symbolically, and linguistically communicate in a single language or in multiple languages. Some people with high levels of verbal and linguistic intelligence are astute enough to derive the general verbal meaning of words from different languages by interpreting their Latin origin. **Interactive intelligence**, a very abstract and highly complex form of intelligence, is the realm of relating basic and functional intelligence to the real world. The definition of interactive intelligence varies by continent, country, province, state, community, gender group, age, socioeconomic group, and ethnic group. Interactive intelligence adds interactive and interpersonal factors to the total combined intelligence indicator. Coping skills, "street smarts," cultural skills, organizational familiarity, and unique social skills are all relevant interactive intelligence factors that should be factored in to any measurement of overall intelligence. **Physiological intelligence** is the ability to run without stumbling, dance with synchronized rhythm, hit a tennis ball, shoot a basketball, swim a lap, precisely cut a tomato, and perform any rhythmic kinesthetic action. Just like a tennis player instinctively knows how to grip a tennis racket to accurately locate a shot, a good basketball player knows how to shoot a basketball with a certain arch and a certain force to maximize the odds that it will go through the hoop. Dancers, on the other hand, instinctively learn new synchronized steps and motions that distinguish them from other dancers. This ability to coordinate pace, motion, rhythm, and physical cadence is truly a unique form of intelligence. As is the case with the other inner drivers, intelligence is a critical component of the pursuit of excellence and continuous improvement. In the absence of rational intelligence, achieving excellence is virtually impossible. While the nine intelligence types have great importance, it is only through the four subfactors that our intelligence can truly manifest itself. These intelligence subfactors, which are shown in the EDGE framework (Figure 3.3), hold the secret to your acquisition and use of the information, skills, knowledge, and insight that arise from your pursuit of intelligence. Let's examine these four subfactors in greater detail.

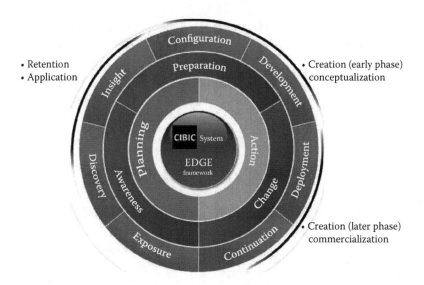

- Retention
- Application

• Creation (early phase) conceptualization

• Creation (later phase) commercialization

Intelligence

The EDGE framework directly promotes the pursuit of intelligence by enhancing learning and development at a fundamental level. By facilitating exposure, retention, application, and creation, the EDGE framework highlights each of the four intelligence subfactors.

Exposure

The subfactor of exposure is highlighted in the first EDGE progression. This progression highlights the great fundamental importance of initial awareness and exposure.

Retention

The subfactor of retention is highlighted in the EDGE framework discovery and insight progressions.

Application

The subfactor of application is highlighted in the EDGE framework in the targeting and development progressions.

Creation

The subfactor of creation is highlighted in the development and deployment progressions. Creation is the specific manifestation of your conceptualization and commercialization endeavors.

FIGURE 3.3
Intelligence and the EDGE framework.

Exposure

When you attend a class, attend a seminar, spend time with a mentor, or attend an information session, you fulfill the first requirement of comprehensive learning: exposure. Exposure and its close precursor of access are the initial steps to acquire knowledge as we know it. Without exposure, retention, application, and creation are impossible. At its basic level, exposure is only possible through the existence of a sensory stimulus; sight, sound, smell, touch, taste, or a sixth sense. When we attend a class, sit in a seminar, spend time with a mentor, or experience any other sensory interactions, our exposure promotes the basic capacity to learn. It is only through this learning that retention, application, and creation become possible or probable. Although exposure promotes the possibility of retention, application, and creation, our individual, group, and organizational decision to accept or reject our exposure stimulus can have a very profound effect on the pursuit of intelligence. Access to the exposure only leads to physical exposure when a conscious decision to accept that exposure is made and embraced. When that conscious decision is made and embraced, the pursuit of intelligence can truly begin. Although some may classify exposure in singular terms, such a generalization promotes widespread danger. While some exposure is good and generally beneficial, other types of exposure can bring with it great danger and harm. While our exposure to some people can be beneficial, our exposure to other people can promote great harm. While our exposure to some physical environments can be beneficial, our exposure to other environments can be harmful. While our exposure to some chemicals and substances can be beneficial, our exposure to other chemicals and substances can be harmful. And while our exposure to some sights, sounds, and smells can be beneficial, our exposure to other sights, sounds, and smells can be harmful. When we truly embrace and comprehend the benefits and risks of the exposure dynamic, we promote the pursuit of intelligence in a manner that promotes and facilitates our true pursuit of excellence.

Retention

Although the importance of exposure can never be understated, the fundamental importance of retention can never be overstated. While the ability to retain, remember, and preserve information is a precious gift, the inability to retain, remember, and otherwise preserve that same information is a cataclysmic waste. Our inability to retain, remember, and otherwise preserve information can erode efficiency, hamper productivity, inhibit progress, and obstruct continuous improvement in its entirety. Be it due to academic cramming, callous disregard, cognitive limitations, or biological degradation, the loss of information, insight, know-how, and wisdom can be dreadful, awful, horrendous, or regrettable depending on the specific circumstances. While some struggle with cognitive inhibitors, and others suffer from neurological inhibitors including Alzheimer's disease, a third group of people suffer from only their unwillingness to retain information. To be willing to learn but unable to learn is sad, but to be able to learn and yet unwilling to learn is tragic. To be exposed to good things is great, but to not retain that information is dreadful, awful, horrendous, and usually regrettable. Without short- and long-term retention, what you read, see, hear, and otherwise gain in the short term will undoubtedly be lost in the long term, robbing you of the potential to achieve excellence in the long term. For those who are willing and able to retain information, the burden of retention lies in the method and approach for retaining that information. Although retention of information is an end goal, the method and approach for promoting that end goal can vary widely. Although CIBIC promotes the use of structure, visualization, acronymization (the use of acronyms), and intonation to maximize retention, an almost endless list of alternate approaches to retention exists. Unfortunately, not all retention methods, approaches, and systems are created equal. While some scholars, leaders, educators, writers, speakers, and elders have become masters at the art of promoting retention, many others have yet to elevate themselves to true retention promoter status. The ability to effectively open the mind of others is a special ability that requires originality, creativity, and efficiency to master. People who are exposed to these masters benefit from the heightened retention that is a natural result of their exposure. As they are highlighted in the CIBIC system, structure, visualization, acronymization, and intonation can undeniably affect retention at the individual and collective levels. Simply consider the impact of intonation to the art of retention. For some, the use of intonation to promote memory and retention is truly noteworthy. For these individuals, the intuitive use of music, tones, harmony, and harmonic repetition to promote the long-term retention of information is truly eye opening. I have personally used music as a memory enhancer since I was a child and other people on other continents have used this same retentive intonation with amazing results. Designated historians from the Dogon Tribe of Mali West Africa currently use the art of retentive intonation to retain 50,000 years of their collective history. This retentive intonation focuses on the retention of ancient stories that highlight their history. This is just one example of how structure, visualization, acronymization, and intonation can be used to promote retention. From advanced concept visualization and visual imprinting to the use of acronyms and phrases, the number of retention-promoting concepts and methods is almost endless. And although we are all governed by natural laws that limit our mass retentive potential, we nonetheless have it in our power to leverage the incredible power of structure, visualization, acronymization, and intonation to more efficiently chronicle our exposures and our experiences. While retention can promote the application of knowledge and the creation of new knowledge, insight, inventions, and intellectual capital, this pursuit is only possible when the proper state of mind exists. As a general rule, when a mind is in turmoil, a mind is in conflict. And, when a mind is in conflict, the creativity that promotes application and creation is severely limited. The sad fact of the matter is that poor living circumstances often interfere with knowledge retention. The basic need to survive forces far too many to live with the specter of perpetual crises. For those who face this specter, addressing this retention and creativity robbing reality must be addressed before the ability to retain can be achieved. Although you should now have a much better understanding of retention as a facilitator of intelligence, your exploration of this subject matter would be wholly incomplete without a discussion of the dynamics of application as a promoter of retention.

Application

While the retention of knowledge can promote skill building, only the application of that knowledge signals true competence. And it is only through this competence that true mastery can occur. When physicians perform procedures, lawyers litigate cases, engineers design products, accountants prepare reports, and students write dissertations, they are each applying their critical skills. And whereas these critical skill sets may vary by profession and pursuit, their use in the pursuit of excellence is undeniable. While accountants must possess mathematical intelligence and botanists must have naturalistic intelligence, other disciplines require different forms of intelligence. Whereas a surgeon may require visual, spatial, naturalistic, and physiological intelligence, a diplomat may require interactive and linguistic intelligence. Regardless of your profession or pursuit, the importance of your ability to apply acquired knowledge should never be understated. Retention without comprehension and creative application will almost never be in your best interest. As a pursuit, the application of knowledge is typically symbolized through your ability and willingness to experiment with, play with, test, validate, rationalize, analyze, interpret, ponder, legitimize, and comprehend information as part of your intuitive process of refined adjustment. Through your commitment to these pursuits, the application of knowledge becomes a likelihood if not a certainty. Once you develop the ability to successfully apply information, skills, knowledge, and insight, you promote your ability to create new standards, products, processes, practices, methods, frameworks, dynamics, and realities.

Creation

While exposure, retention, and application are major subfactors of intelligence, only creation exceeds them all. It is only through your creative originality that your pursuit of excellence can truly succeed. Creation is the art, practice, or endeavor of developing the new concepts, ideas, standards, products, processes, practices, methods, frameworks, dynamics, and realities that promote a better tomorrow. It is only through creation and development that you can vanquish the status quo. Legal scholars, medical researchers, custom software programmers, leading edge surgeons, developmental chemists, entrepreneurs, philosophers, architects, research botanists, and many astrophysicists all embrace creation to promote their hopes for a better tomorrow. Through creation, the void of today's uncertainties changes into the details of tomorrow's opportunities. It is through your vision, precision, insight, and ingenuity that our hopes for tomorrow will spring eternal. Don't be misled, however, because the ability to create is no easy task. Those who create can face a wide range of challenges. From unanticipated medical complications to faulty design, new concepts, ideas, standards, products, processes, practices, methods, frameworks, dynamics, and realities can invariably spawn new risks that those who create must address. And even when these risks are addressed, other challenges often loom in the distance. New concepts, ideas, standards, products, processes, practices, methods, and frameworks often need other new concepts, ideas, standards, products, processes, practices, methods, and frameworks to be successfully launched. As such, those who create must always be aware that creation promotes creation, and creation requires creation.

Despite these challenges, those who possess the ability to create truly possess a gift to be cherished. While some may think that the presence and pursuit of intelligence are somehow distinct from the EDGE framework, such an interpretation has no basis in fact. In fact, the pursuit of intelligence as an activity is directly described in the EDGE framework. As a scalable and universal development, learning, and change-promoting framework, the EDGE framework is fully adaptable to all activities related to the pursuit of excellence and continuous improvement. That scalability and universal applicability help to guarantee and solidify EDGE framework use in all of your chosen endeavors.

Genius Is Talent Set On Fire by Courage.

HENRY VAN DYKE

Intelligence Is the Ability to Adapt to Change.

STEPHEN HAWKING

RESILIENCE

Resilience is the ability to overcome the setbacks and disappointments that impede and obstruct the pursuit of excellence. Resilience is the strength of character to overcome misfortune, and power of will to succeed in the face of utter devastation. When the weak spirited crumble, the resilient always rise to the occasion. In the pursuit of excellence and continuous improvement, there is simply no substitute for the power of resilience. And while the pursuit of excellence can be sometimes gut wrenching and occasionally agonizing, the strong learn that these realities are just part of life. Unless you live in an existential vacuum, adversity will always be a part of life. And while some view adversity as self-originated and self-correcting, the true reality is that adversity is best faced with vision, discipline, determination, and reinforcement, the four subfactors of resilience. While some consider adversity a one-dimensional phenomenon, that perspective has no basis. Adversity, in classic terms, manifests itself from your social, economic, psychological, physiological, environmental, technical, chronological, performance, and biological–chemical–pharmaceutical realities, previously referred to as your nine chaos designation types. By focusing your pursuit of resilience on the nine chaos designation types, we create a mechanism for combating chaos through the power of your own resilience. Just like you use resilience to combat chaos, you can also use resilience to help you address and manage the basic raw emotions that can influence your chaotic landscape. The sorrow, malaise, uncertainty, skepticism, and doubt that can often cloud your realities are truly no match for the power of resilience. And while these antagonists and raw emotions are sometimes the manifestation of your outer realities and sometimes the manifestation of your inner realities, their existence almost always influences our pursuit of excellence. It is only through the power of resilience that we can vanquish these antagonists and raw emotions to their rightful place; the void of insignificance. To sulk or mourn is to be human, but to continually dwell in that sorrow is never in your best interest or the best interest of others. We must always rise above our sorrows and embrace the vision of a brighter tomorrow. It is from the depths of our sorrows that we can achieve our most noteworthy achievements. Friedrich Nietzsche once stated, "What doesn't kill us, makes us stronger," and King Solomon stated, "This too shall pass," in specific reference to the debilitating influence that pain, disappointment, despair, hardship, and sorrow have on the human psyche. While these experiences almost always leave behind a scar or two, they also make you stronger and more resilient, better able to face the challenges ahead. While embracing resilience can promote your pursuits, only a thorough understanding of the subfactors of resilience can guarantee those pursuits. This understanding begins by understanding the importance of vision in the pursuit of resilience.

Vision

In the earlier chapter on planning, the importance of vision and its role in mission determination were discussed in great detail. While that discussion should have promoted your planning prowess, it did not address the almost certain emergence of adversity in the planning and implementation process. It is in your darkest hours that you will truly come to understand the importance of vision in the pursuit of your goals. When you invariably encounter "the brick wall" that impedes your goal-driven pursuits, you may be left wondering why you chose a specific objective. In the absence of a clearly crafted vision, it may be difficult if not impossible for you to answer the question of why a specific objective was chosen, leaving you frustrated and uncertain about your next step. The ever-present and menacing nature of adversity, gaps, and barriers tends to wear down even those with the strongest of character. When you possess a clear vision and the resolve to see that vision through, those adversity, gaps, and barriers become a little less menacing and a lot less prevalent. The Dalai Lama once stated that "In order to carry a positive action, we must develop here a positive vision." It is only from our vision that your life energy and our resilience spring eternal. That life energy is magnified in the presence of discipline.

Discipline

If your vision is critical for promoting resilience, then your discipline is essential. Your discipline represents your tendency and propensity for adhering to a predetermined course of action to pursue an objective. While resolving adversities, eliminating gaps, and navigating barriers are essential to your pursuits, only your discipline can guarantee that pursuit. There is simply no substitute for discipline in promoting a better tomorrow. Discipline promotes regimen, regimen promotes progress, and progress promotes the pursuit of excellence. While your regimen may include embracing high standards and best practices, your regimen may also include following a predetermined series of steps or a predetermined schedule. Regardless of your specific realities, your commitment to your regimen holds great importance. Your words and promises mean nothing without your full commitment to embrace a chosen pursuit. And without the discipline to follow through, your commitment means nothing. Without discipline, your hopes, dreams, and desires will almost certainly fade into oblivion. Although some people define discipline as following a consistent schedule, and others define discipline as the tendency to be stubbornly inflexible, for purposes of this subject matter, discipline is the practice of embracing and pursuing a consistent milestone inclusive path forward. While it would be easy to condense the discussion of discipline to a purely singular individual discussion, the fact of the matter is that discipline is often the manifestation of plural circumstances. President George Washington once stated that "Discipline is the soul of an army. It makes small numbers formidable; procures success to the weak, and esteem to all." As such, it's important for you to recognize that discipline can manifest itself singularly and collectively. While discipline is truly a critical pursuit, only your determination can help you to solidify this pursuit.

Determination

While resilience promotes excellence, and discipline promotes resilience, only your determination can promote your discipline. And while discipline highlights sequence, determination highlights resolve. In classic terms, your determination is your ability to eliminate, resolve, and overcome adversity and setbacks. While these adversities and setbacks always loom in the distance, only your determination promotes their elimination and resolution. The power of determination is undebatable, unquestionable, and undeniable. It is through determination that the unqualified rise to become the qualified, the represented rise to become the representors, and the followers rise to become the leaders. Without determination, our dreams will never come true and our hopes will never be fulfilled. The power to rise up, overcome, prevail, and succeed rises from the power of determination. Those who seek the power to prevail must first seek determination to achieve. While some consider determination as the act or process of being stubborn, that is not always the case. There is a thin line between stubborn disregard and focused determination. While stubborn disregard promotes the status quo, focused determination highlights change as a precursor of excellence and the willingness to endure the unimaginable in pursuit of a better tomorrow. Although vision, discipline, and determination promote a better tomorrow, only reinforcement augments that pursuit.

Reinforcement

In classic terms, reinforcement is the process of securing, augmenting, or supplementing a behavior, mechanism, process, or framework. While builders reinforce foundations or walls, CIBIC enthusiasts reinforce healthy habits, positive pursuits, critical endeavors, and essential activities. While your initial reinforcement endeavors may focus on individual endeavors, make no mistake, the endeavor of reinforcement is just as much a collective endeavor as it is a singular endeavor. Be it through singular commitment or collective action, the reinforcement endeavor can be both uplifting and awe-inspiring. The singular or collective impact of repetition, collaboration, dependency, and co-dependency can create reinforcing mechanisms that promote the pursuit of excellence at all levels. This collective power, which we will hereafter refer to as HERD power, helps to reinforce the change that promotes our pursuit of excellence. HERD, which is an acronym for **h**abit, **e**ngagement, **r**eward, and **d**ependency, describes the power behind your reinforcing endeavors. Like a thundering herd of bison, HERD power helps you to promote and solidify resilience by establishing a strong collaborative stimulus for reinforcing resilience. There is no greater reinforcing mechanism than the power of habitual consistency, the potential of shared vision, the joy of being rewarded, and the strength of collaboration. **HERD** power helps you to prevail in the face of adversity, helps you to succeed despite the circumstances, and helps you to rise up in the face of devastation. As is the case with most things in nature, the whole is generally equal to the sum of the parts. In the case of HERD power, the engagement and dependency supporting mechanisms promote the group influence factors of reinforcement. When your forward positive pursuits are widely embraced, and shared by others, the success of those pursuits is usually magnified. The greater the number of people that cheer you on, the greater the success of your chosen endeavor.

Success Is 99 Percent Failure.

SOICHIRO HONDA

Without a Struggle, There Can Be No Progress.

FREDERICK DOUGLASS

ENTHUSIASM

In the realm of our existence, some things are predictable and some things are controllable. And while our ability to pursue our goals is often predictable, and our desire to pursue those goals is often controllable, the pursuit of our mission still has its challenges. The great motivational psychologist Abraham Maslow once stated, "What a man can be, he should be. We call this self-actualization." While our pursuit of self-actualization is generally within the realm of what we can control, our ability to achieve self-actualization is significantly influenced by our ability to create enthusiasm for this pursuit, individually and collectively. As such, your willingness, ability, and propensity for creating enthusiasm have great profound importance in the pursuit of continuous improvement. Enthusiasm represents your ability to create eagerness, fervor, passion, and vigor for supporting a chosen pursuit. The passion that fuels our pursuit of excellence and continuous improvement rises from the infinitum of our enthusiasm. Boundless in magnitude and limitless in influence, your enthusiasm is the fire that creates possibilities out of what was previously impossible. While some view the manifestation of enthusiasm as unidimensional, that view is far from reality. Enthusiasm is the manifestation of physiology, psychology, motivation, and gratification. You must have the physiology to perform, the psychology to care, the motivation to succeed, and the mechanism to be gratified before enthusiasm can exist, prosper, and thrive. In the absence of any of the four, your ability to become enthusiastic wanes and declines. As important as physiology, psychology, motivation, and gratification are in the pursuit of enthusiasm, rationality and viability loom just as large. While rationality applies to the sensibility aspect of your pursuits, viability applies to the achievability aspect of those same pursuits. While we each have it in our power to choose our given pursuits, the sensibility of those pursuits is not always guaranteed. Although the endeavor of planning helps to promote sensible pursuit, that pursuit does not always guarantee that our pursuits will be deemed as truly sensible in the final analysis. When the sensibility of our chosen pursuits is thrown into question, the enthusiasm for that chosen pursuit can and most likely will wane. The viability question presents some of the same considerations as the sensibility question. While many of us regularly ponder the question of viability in our chosen pursuits, our thoughts alone are generally not enough to render our concerns about viability irrelevant. Ever-changing reality dynamics tend to make the selection of viable pursuits an increasingly difficult endeavor. However, when our chosen endeavors are both sensible and viable, our ability to create, promote, and sustain enthusiasm should always exist. While the existence or sensibility and viability always helps to create, promote, and sustain enthusiasm, creating that enthusiasm also requires a careful approach to the physiology, psychology, motivation, and gratification subject matter. Physiology, as a gap and chaotic factor component, directly highlights the role that handicaps, physical conditions, physical age, or other physical limitations play in the pursuit of enthusiasm. Psychology, as a gap and chaotic factors component, highlights the role cognitive disorders and cognitive limitations play in the pursuit of enthusiasm. Physiology and psychology highlight our general capacity to be enthusiastic about a chosen course of action. On the other hand, motivation and gratification highlight the associated mechanisms for encouraging action or change when the capacity for action or change exists. In the next sections, beginning with the narrative of physiology, we will discuss each of the four subfactors in expanded detail.

Physiology

In the realm of enthusiasm, your ability to meet or exceed your physical demands will often influence your pursuit of excellence. Your physiology or lack thereof determines your physical capacity. Physiology is a science that deals with the ways that living things function.

> phys·i·ol·o·gy *noun*\ ˌfi-zē-'ä-lə-jē\: 1. a science that deals with the ways that living things function; 2. the ways that living things or any of their parts function.

Even with its nuances, the dynamics of physiology are easy to highlight and easy to comprehend. While many of us have the option of improving our physiology through basic health maintenance, dieting, healthy living, and aerobic conditioning, that choice is not always universally embraced and pursued. For those who choose to create enthusiasm through improved physiology, the future holds great promise. When you improve your fitness level, you improve your health, and when you improve your health, you improve your outlook. But while your physiology is critical to the creation of enthusiasm, psychology is equally important.

Psychology

In the realm of enthusiasm, your psychological or mental prowess can often fuel your pursuit of excellence. Psychologist Edward Thorndike once stated that "psychology helps to measure the probability that an aim is attainable." No matter what your perspective is, psychology always controls your outlook, your world, and your realities. Commonly known as the study of the mind and behavior, psychology plays a major role in the creation and sustainability of enthusiasm.

> psy·chol·o·gy *noun*: 1. the science or study of the mind and behavior; 2. the way a person or group thinks.

While some would argue that psychology pales in comparison to physiology as a predominant promoter of enthusiasm, I would beg to differ. Without the power of the mind, there can be no stimulus to improve, no wisdom to focus, no energy to perform, and no motivation to grow. And while some believe that creating mental and cognitive enthusiasm is always within the realm of possibilities for everyone, that view has no basis in fact. In fact, with 18.6% of the population suffering from mental illness of one form or another, the ability to create and sustain enthusiasm should never be considered a given. While your physiology and psychology promote the existence of enthusiasm, only motivation and gratification can reinforce and sustain that enthusiasm.

Motivation

Your dreams, your vision, your desires, and your goals only exist when the motivation to succeed also exists. While some view motivation in simplistic terms, others learn that motivation is truly a complex pursuit. Motivation is the act or process of giving someone a reason for doing something.

> mo·ti·va·tion *noun*\ˌmō-tə-ˈvā-shən\: 1. the act or process of giving some-one a reason for doing something; 2. the act or process of motivating some-one; 3. the condition of being eager to act or work; 4. the condition of being motivated; 5. a force or influence that causes someone to do something.

Without motivation, there is no desire; without desire, there is no work; without work, there is no achievement; and without achievement, there is no success. In the realm of psychology, motivation rules supreme. Some of the brightest motivational scholars from B.F. Skinner to Abraham Maslow spent their life working to understand and document the dynamics of motivation. Although motivation is the fuel that inspires progress, gratification is the dynamic that rewards that progress.

Gratification

Motivation inspires and gratification rewards. In the absence of gratification, long-term progress and sustainability are greatly diminished. Without gratification, our hopes for a better tomorrow remain just that, hopes. Gratification is defined as pleasure, especially when gained from the satisfaction of a desire.

> grat·i·fi·ca·tion *noun*\gratəfi'kāSHən\: 1. pleasure, especially when gained from the satisfaction of a desire.

Although some may classify gratification in singular terms, gratification is more dynamic than most people would think. There are literally a thousand different types of gratification ranging from pay for work to receiving a birthday or holiday gift. Other forms of gratification include things as small as receiving a piece of cake to receiving a flower delivery. Gratification also has a special time dynamic that is growing in prevalence. While delayed gratification used to be a widely accepted norm, instant gratification has greatly increased in preference, especially among millennials. Although instant gratification has greatly increased in prevalence, it has also sadly ushered in a new era of entitlement expectations that is eroding our societal fabric. Although earned instant gratification is beneficial in many ways, unearned instant gratification is generally detrimental on many levels.

What a Man Can Be, He Should Be. We Call This Self-Actualization.

ABRAHAM MASLOW

The Energy of the Mind Is the Essence of Life.

ARISTOTLE

SUSTAINABILITY

As both an inner driver and an outer quality, there is absolutely, positively, no substitute for sustainability. While the first inner driver of stability is a state, the final inner driver of sustainability is a continuum. For those who understand that success is a journey and not a destination, sustainability is both critical and essential. For both individual and collective interests, sustainability turns the success of today into the successes of tomorrow, and the hopes of today into the certainties of tomorrow. Deemed a second thought by some and an afterthought by others, sustainability is neither a second thought nor an afterthought. In CIBIC, sustainability extends shorter-term efforts into longer-term gains. Sustainability perpetuates these longer-term gains by highlighting safety, security, reliability, and quality as the dominant promoters of excellence. As was the case with the other inner drivers, only your comprehension of the four subfactors of sustainability can promote the pursuit of excellence. **Safety** relates to your ability to promote sustainability through the reduction of the harm, destruction, damage, and devastation that plagues life, performance, achievement, and continuity. Generally referred to as life safety, safety is the most critical element of sustainability. **Security** relates to your ability to promote sustainability through the elimination of the loss, displacement, incursion, and disruption that threatens assets, resources, capabilities, and bandwidth. Generally referred to as resource security, security has been increasingly embraced by individual and collective interests as a means of addressing the cyber security and terrorism issues that continue to plague society. The final two sustainability subfactors, although not as critical, are nonetheless profoundly important to the pursuit of sustainability. **Reliability** relates to your ability to promote sustainability through your behavior, practices, standards, and values; promoting consistency and perpetuity. And finally, **quality** relates to your ability to promote sustainability through higher levels of precision, craftsmanship, creativity, innovation, and professionalism. Together, these four pursuits and subfactors promote, perpetuate, and bolster sustainability at all levels. Rather than focusing on behavior, these four subfactors highlight the attributes that perpetuate and solidify the sustainability continuum.

Safety

As we discussed earlier, safety relates to your ability to individually and collectively reduce or eliminate the risk of harm, destruction, damage, and devastation that affects life, performance, achievement, and continuity. As an endeavor, safety is the practice of using predetermined methods, standards, and practices to eliminate the potential for harm, destruction, damage, and devastation. This endeavor is critically important to individual and collective interests because of its role in protecting life, liberty, and the pursuit of happiness. Even with its critical importance, safety as an endeavor enjoys less than universal acceptance. Limited self-interests, personal biases, and callous disregard still promote the everyday loss of life and human potential that plagues society. Although history and our personal experiences have taught us otherwise, we continue to make some of the same safety compromising mistakes repetitively, perpetuating the same nightmares over and over again. And while various government and public sector agencies and institutions have advanced the cause of public safety through their rules and regulations, these rules and regulations have only marginally improved public safety. Even in the midst of active intervention, occupational, food, drug, product, chemical, health, transportation, and environmental safety remains an elusive goal. While this active intervention is a good first step toward public safety, one important step remains: our personal active involvement. We each are undeniably responsible for promoting safety in our active endeavors, both individual and collective. Even when our biases and contrary interests interfere with the pursuit of safety, we are still nonetheless responsible for promoting safety mechanisms and practices. By promoting occupational, food, drug, product, chemical, health, transportation, and environmental safety among other safety endeavors, we promote the mechanisms and practices that promote a truly safe environment for us all. While safety begins with your desire, it ends with your awareness of your surroundings and circumstances. In the absence of this awareness, tragedies happen. While the loss of life and human potential is always sad, the "avoidable" loss of life and human potential is both unconscionable and tragic. Only your active pursuit of safety can prevent these unconscionable and tragic things from happening.

Security

As we also discussed earlier, security relates to your ability to address and eliminate the risk of theft, displacement, incursion, and disruption that threatens assets, resources, capabilities, and bandwidth. As an endeavor, security is the practice of using predetermined methods, standards, and practices to mitigate the risk of theft, displacement, incursion, and disruption among other threats. Security also represents our endeavors to preserve, protect, defend, and perpetuate our resources and collective best interests including life, liberty, and the pursuit of happiness. Although protecting life is a critical pursuit, promoting security is just as important. By promoting security, we help to protect, safeguard, secure, and shield against the loss of assets, resources, bandwidth, and capabilities that are often the target of miscreants, terrorist, demagogues, and rogue interests. While some people think of security as the purchase and use of theft protection systems, that definition only describes a very small subsegment of the overall security endeavor. Security as an endeavor includes theft loss prevention, intellectual property loss prevention, data loss prevention, perimeter security protection, sensitive information safeguarding, and intrusion protection among other endeavors. Security preservation, protection, and defense resources include but are not limited to the military, the central intelligence complex, security systems, security devices, patents, copyrights, trademarks, and trade names among other resources. And while the masses may recognize public entities, regional interests, and niche security service entities as the de facto providers of security-promoting products, solutions, capabilities, and resources, we each have the individual and collective responsibility to promote the pursuit of security in our everyday endeavors. When we experience the loss of assets, resources, bandwidth, and capabilities, the ramifications to our ability to continue and sustain our chosen pursuits are many times damaged and compromised, sometimes beyond the point of recovery. As such, we must all be mindful of our surroundings and take the necessary steps to promote a secure living, work, and natural environment.

Reliability

Reliability represents the methods and practices that promote sustainability and other uptime enhancing qualities. By promoting both confidence and continuity, reliability is a truly critical element of sustainability. Renowned computer scientist Edsger Wybe Dijkstra was once quoted as saying "simplicity is a prerequisite for reliability." At a fundamental level, Dijkstra couldn't have said it better. Reliability promotes sustainability by perpetuating control, reason, logic, and simplicity. Without reliability, sustainability is unlikely, and without sustainability, you may not be able to prove your reliability. Although some view reliability as a time-driven dynamic, that view is limited at best. In broader, more applicable terms, reliability highlights your ability to reliably meet a variety of time, quality, safety, uptime, and delivery-based performance standards. While reliability is often the manifestation of your behavior, practices, standards, and values, it can also be the manifestation of your ability to meet or exceed prevailing expectations as designated by your peers, clients, associates, and intermediaries. Regardless of your specific realities, reliability will almost always promote your success and the pursuit of a better tomorrow. When we improve our reliability, we ultimately build the trust, admiration, goodwill, and affinity that will always promote the pursuit of excellence.

Quality

While safety, security, and reliability are critical, they pale in comparison to the pursuit of quality. In the absence of quality, safety, security, and reliability are improbable, impossible, and highly unlikely. Quality as a practice is the pursuit of precision, craftsmanship, and professionalism as the critical precursor of value. Quality as a philosophy is the pursuit of perfection through our endeavors to embrace sustainable continuity. While some define quality in terms of the various quality standards that exist, that definition is limited at best. Although ISO, Six Sigma, and the countless other quality standards can help to promote quality, in the final analysis, only your tireless pursuit of precision, craftsmanship, and professionalism, individually and collectively, can promote quality. Quality is almost always the manifestation of your behaviors, practices, standards, and values that promote precision, craftsmanship, innovation, and professionalism. Quality is also about embracing the pursuit of perfection in our daily endeavors; rejecting mediocrity as an acceptable outcome and rejecting failure as even a remote possibility. In the final outcome, when safety, security, reliability, and quality spring eternal, sustainability will always flourish. Your challenge is to embrace the notion that actions speak louder than words by embracing the pursuit of sustainability in all of your endeavors. When we all embrace this pursuit enthusiastically and relentlessly, excellence will almost always prevail.

The Safety of the People Shall Be the Highest Law.

CICERO

The Flame That Shines Twice as Bright, Burns Half as Long.

LAO TZU

DYNAMIC ANALYTICS

For every action, there is always a proportional reaction of some sort. In CIBIC, a change in one dynamic will almost invariably affect other dynamics. That means a change in your inner drivers will almost always affect your outer qualities, and vice versa. Such is the reality of continuous improvement. In CIBIC, dynamic analytics is the process of quantifying and qualifying inner driver and outer qualities' strengths through visualization, assessment, and analysis. It is only through dynamic analytics that you can build a true understanding of your relative strengths or lack thereof. In CIBIC, dynamic analytics follows a three-step process: visual mapping, strength assessment, and strength visualization. **Visual mapping** is the process of mapping and organizing inner drivers and outer qualities to promote a better understanding of their reciprocal connectivity. **Strength assessment** is the process of using active surveys and assessments to determine a numeric strength index for each inner driver. And finally, **strength visualization** is the process of visually mapping inner driver strength using a circular mapping grid. Dynamic analytics as a process is designed to promote greater comprehension of the downstream configuration, expectations management, development, deployment, and change subject matters that we will cover in later chapters. By building a greater understanding of the dynamic analytics process, beginning with visual mapping, the pursuit of excellence and continuous improvement becomes a much easier endeavor.

Visual Mapping

As we discussed earlier, visual mapping is the process of representing the inner drivers and outer qualities in a manner that promotes downstream configuration, development, and deployment. Visually, the nine inner drivers and outer qualities are graphically organized using the CIBIC Cognitive Dynamics Sphere. The Cognitive Dynamics Sphere segments drivers and qualities into two balanced hemispheres: the left hemisphere for drivers and the right hemisphere for qualities. Just like the human cognitive system is elegantly organized into right and left hemispheres, the CIBIC Cognitive Dynamics Sphere is also organized hemispherically, as shown in Figure 3.4, to promote easier comprehension and efficiency. By highlighting the structural connectivity between drivers and qualities,

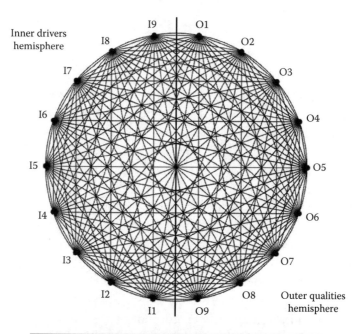

Designation	Description	Designation	Description
I1	Stability	O1	Convenience
I2	Adaptability	O2	Opinions
I3	Planning	O3	Motivations
I4	Patience	O4	Proficiencies
I5	Humility	O5	Output
I6	Intelligence	O6	Sustainability
I7	Resilience	O7	Influences
I8	Enthusiasm	O8	Timeliness
I9	Sustainability	O9	Economics

FIGURE 3.4
The CIBIC Cognitive Dynamics Sphere.

the CIBIC cognitive dynamics system helps to promote greater comprehension of CIBIC at a much higher level, promoting both continuous improvement and excellence.

This structured approach highlights the great profound importance of the inner drivers and outer qualities, and the connectivity risks that always reign supreme. In the practical world, each driver, attribute, competency, and quality is invariably linked to the other drivers, attributes, competencies, and qualities, individually, collectively, and vice versa. In the inner driver realm, this connectivity has even greater prominence. In general terms, the measured change of one inner driver almost always leads to a proportional change of the other inner drivers, and vice versa.

When your stability wanes either by choice or external influences, the corresponding level of adaptability, planning, patience, humility, intelligence, resilience, enthusiasm, and sustainability also wanes. Correspondingly, when adaptability wanes as a result of direct or indirect causes, stability, planning, patience, humility, intelligence, resilience, enthusiasm, and sustainability also wane, either immediately or latently. This same connectivity applies equally to each of the inner drivers and their subfactors. As such, in CIBIC, mediocrity or failure in one area almost always translates into mediocrity or failure in other areas. While each inner driver influences the other inner drivers, they also influence the nine outer qualities, either exclusively or in tandem with the other inner drivers. Just like our inner power promotes our outer strength, the inner drivers influence the outer qualities, and vice versa. Alternatively, weakness or deficiency in one CIBIC area or hemisphere will generally promote weakness or deficiency in other CIBIC areas or hemispheres. In the CIBIC, being well rounded is not only critical, it is essential. For the span of my years, the term *well rounded* has been used and embraced to promote the value of good balance. Although this term has been widely used, I never knew the exact meaning of being well rounded in very specific terms. CIBIC answers this age-old question in very specific terms. Once you understand the nuances of visual mapping, the strength assessment and quantification subject matter gains much greater importance.

Active Strength Assessment

To know, and not measure, is a critical error. Such is the importance of active strength assessment. While inner driver awareness can promote your pursuits, only inner driver measurement can fuel that pursuit. And while your pursuit of excellence may manifest itself in different ways, it is ultimately your ability to measure and interpret that pursuit that holds great importance. In CIBIC, inner driver measurement is accomplished using the Inner Driver Assessment Tool, also known as the Inner Driver Survey. The Inner Driver Survey, as shown in Figure 3.5, highlights the use of a scaled response survey tool to gauge specific strengths in the nine inner driver categories.

This survey uses a non-disguised question-and-answer format to simplistically gauge inner driver subfactor strength. These gauged strength assessments are used to determine your overall strength in the nine inner driver categories. While each subfactor is approximated using a 0 to 100 scale for estimated strength, each inner driver is approximated using a 0

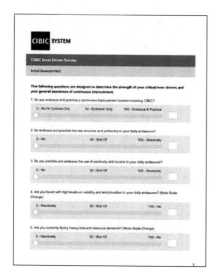

IDS - self
Inner driver
self-assessment survey

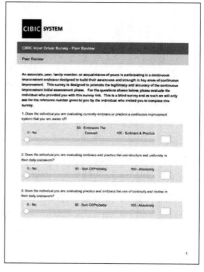

IDS - peer
Inner driver
peer review survey

FIGURE 3.5
Inner driver self-assessment and peer surveys.

to 400 scale. Inner driver ratings of 300 or higher typically reflect average to strong inner driver strength, while ratings below 200 reflect generally weak inner driver strength. While your self-assessment of inner driver strength is a natural first step, care must be taken to ensure that these measured assessments truly convey real-world realities. To promote the pursuit of truly relative information, the peer review survey was added to the strength assessment process. In the peer review process, the same inner driver assessment surveying is performed with other individuals and collective interests with relative knowledge of the survey process participant.

This additional peer review process greatly improves the validity of the strength assessment process. While numerical assessments suffice for some, visual assessments are preferred by others, providing the basis for conscientious reflection and development. While measurement and quantification promote the pursuit of excellence and continuous improvement, only your conceptual understanding of this information will aid you in this pursuit. Active strength visualization promotes this pursuit through the active visualization of inner driver strength dynamics.

Active Strength Visualization

There is simply no substitute for data visualization and active data representation. In CIBIC, the chosen tool for inner driver strength visualization is the FIRM Diagram. The FIRM Diagram, which is an acronym for Freeman Intuitive Radial Measurement, is a visual tool that promotes the pursuit of excellence and continuous improvement by visually highlighting inner driver strength using an easy-to-interpret circular format. By visually representing inner driver strength using this circular format, the FIRM Diagram provides the basis of effective strength visualization and collective comparison. The FIRM Diagram complements the CIBIC Cognitive Dynamics Sphere by providing the numerical basis for each of the 18 cognitive dynamic points; your inner drivers and outer qualities. The FIRM Macro and Micro Diagrams, which are highlighted in Figure 3.6, graphically represent the strength of each inner driver in general or refined terms. The FIRM Macro Diagram visually highlights each of the nine inner drivers in a circular format that visualizes your strength in each of the nine categories.

The FIRM Micro Diagram, on the other hand, visually highlights each of the 36 subfactors in a circular linear format that visualizes your strength in each of the 36 categories. While symmetrical and circular diagrams indicate the presence of good balance, irregular diagrams typically indicate skewed attributes with significant irregularities. By promoting well-rounded balance, the CIBIC system and the FIRM Diagram promote the pursuit of excellence through consistency and versatility.

Variance and Risk

In the dynamic analytics realm, one general rule applies: the greater the variance, the greater the risk. And while some may turn a blind eye to

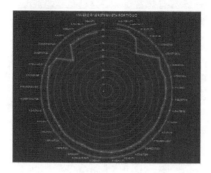

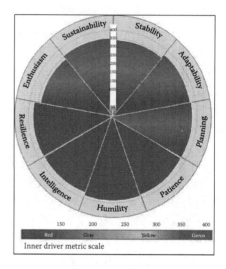

Macro firm diagram

FIGURE 3.6
Inner driver strength and the FIRM Diagram.

variance and deviance as an area of concern, such a decision is risky at best. In CIBIC, variance represents the measured reduction in maximum inner driver strength as determined using the Inner Driver Survey. The greater your inner driver variance, the greater the risk of mediocrity or failure. While many view variance as a singular phenomenon, that is generally never the case. Two types of variances are typically seen in our everyday endeavors: natural variances and impaired variances. When prevailing variances are the manifestation of non-malicious circumstances, they are called natural variances. However, when prevailing variances are the manifestation of malicious circumstances, they are called impaired variances. While natural variances can often be resolved naturally using CIBIC, impaired variances are much more difficult to resolve naturally. As we indirectly alluded to in the adaptability chapter, impaired variances are generally the manifestation of the corrupting influence of destroyers and contaminators. While the "just this once" and "it'll be okay for now" nonchalance from our family, friends, and peers are often at the root of our corrupting interactions, we must each nonetheless accept personal responsibility for the damage that we create through our interactions.

Synopsis

While the importance of dynamic analytics should be generally obvious, that is not always the case. Naivete and a general lack of awareness lead far too many to discount, disregard, and dismiss the importance of metrics and analytics in the pursuit of excellence and continuous improvement. While the timing and relativity of dynamic analytics can vary from person to person, these linkages will invariably and perpetually influence your pursuit of excellence in one way or another. While the lack of adaptability, for instance, may or may not affect your pursuit of excellence in the near term, it will most certainly affect that pursuit in the long term. This same reality applies to each of the inner drivers and outer qualities. And while it is true that the live and let live laissez-faire approach to continuous improvement and the pursuit of excellence appeals to many, this approach always has a cost, either immediately or latently. For this and other reasons, dynamic analytics will always be important to your pursuit of excellence. Be it to promote excellence, development, expectation management, or change, the importance of dynamic analytics is essential, vital, and critical. By helping to promote greater stability, adaptability, planning, patience, humility, intelligence, resilience, enthusiasm, and sustainability, dynamic analytics has great power and importance. And as you will come to understand in the next chapter on the Outer Qualities, dynamic analytics can also greatly influence the strength of your outer qualities.

The Measure of Who We Are Is What We Do with What We Have.

VINCE LOMBARDI

Trust, but Verify.

RONALD REAGAN

4

Understanding the Outer Qualities

Who we are on the inside doesn't always equate to what we are on the outside, and vice versa. Thus far, during our journey into CIBIC, we have discussed the nine inner drivers and the 36 subfactors that influence your life, your realities, and your chosen pursuits. Unquestionable in importance and undeniable in prominence, these inner drivers form the foundation of your inner persona. Although many believe that who you are on the inside directly determines who we are on the outside, the truth of the matter is, the dynamic of inner–outer transference is truly not an exact science. We are individually and collectively the sum of our unique experiences and circumstances. These experiences and circumstances are influenced by our genetics, our environment, and our chosen or predetermined realities. Within these realities, your ability to develop and construct your outer persona and outer qualities is always in a state of flux, influenced by these far-reaching circumstances. As such, it is ultimately your ability to recognize, comprehend, and develop your outer persona and outer qualities that will determine your level of success or lack thereof in your chosen pursuits. This recognition, comprehension, and development begin with an itemization of the very dynamic outer qualities. The outer qualities delineate and highlight the definable outer attributes that describe our visible identity as seen by the outside world. These outer qualities, individually and collectively, form the basis of the expectation and change dynamic that we will discuss further in later chapters. The outer qualities fit into three specific descriptive categories: performance, benefit, and interactive qualities. The performance qualities include the three outer qualities that promote our performance-driven pursuit of excellence: proficiency, output, and sustainability. The benefit qualities include the three outer qualities that support our benefit-driven pursuit of excellence: economics, timeliness, and convenience. The interactive qualities include the three outer qualities that influence our interaction-driven pursuit of excellence: motivations, opinions, and influences. In a manner consistent with our use of acronyms to describe the nine inner drivers, a new acronym was created to highlight the nine outer qualities. The COMPOSITE acronym highlights the nine outer qualities in their corresponding order: convenience, opinions, motivations, proficiencies, output, sustainability, influences, timeliness, and economics. As we discussed earlier, the use of acronyms is widely embraced in CIBIC to promote enhanced learning and longer-term retention. Although we examined the inner drivers earlier using a comprehensive approach, the dynamic nature of the outer qualities lends itself to a completely different approach. Outer qualities dynamics coupled with constantly changing expectation and change management considerations introduce a number of new considerations into the outer qualities subject matter. These new considerations highlight

Outer qualities (COMPOSITE)

Convenience
• Access
• Location
• Approachability
• Usability

Opinions
• Perceptions
• Views
• Values
• Attitudes

Motivations
• Obligations
• Responsibilities
• Accountabilities
• Commitments

Proficiency
• Precision (skill)
• Efficiency
• Creativity
• Familiarity

Output
• Production
• Volume
• Capacity
• Yield

Sustainability
• Continuity
• Perpetuity
• Regularity
• Conservation

Influences
• Networks
• Affiliations
• Collaborations
• Relationships

Timeliness
• Reliability
• Punctuality
• Earliness
• Speediness

Economics
• Compensation
• Cost
• Price
• Value

FIGURE 4.1
Your outer DNA—outer qualities and subfactors.

the vast number of situational uncertainties that exist, easily threatening the integrity of any precisely structured system. As such, to promote the pursuit of excellence, the outer qualities subject matter was developed in general terms and not specific terms as was the case with the inner drivers. Instead of using a very precisely structured narrative to describe the outer qualities, CIBIC uses a very basic narrative to describe each outer driver, promoting the inclusion of situational and industry specific white papers at a later date. Recognizing this chosen approach, each of the nine outer qualities are highlighted below and visualized in Figure 4.1.

CONVENIENCE (A BENEFIT QUALITY)

The first outer quality of Convenience, as described by your access, location, approachability, and usability, highlights your ability to individually or collectively meet convenience expectations that exist with family members, peers, clients, and other interests. Convenience highlights your ability to use, leverage, or otherwise exploit location, proximity, presence, approachability, usability, and access or the lack thereof to promote the pursuit of a desired outcome. For singular and collective interests, this quality can, and often will, influence general decision making and preference at a critical level. Convenience influences a wide variety of decisions ranging from buying decisions to hiring, brand preference, and usability decisions. As is the case with the other outer drivers, the convenience dynamic is heavily influenced by each of the other inner drivers, outer qualities, and the reciprocal connectivity that exists naturally in the CIBIC system.

OPINIONS (AN INTERACTIVE QUALITY)

The second outer quality of Opinions, as described by the perception, view, value, and attitude dynamics, highlights your ability to individually or collectively meet the opinions and general preferences of family members, peers, clients, and other interests. Opinions highlight the importance of perceptions, views, values, and attitudes in the pursuit of a desired outcome. As a describer of both your prevailing posture and your expectations, opinions can influence decision making at highly cognitive levels. While your opinions can influence your actions, they can also influence the actions of others, when they are shared with others actively or passively. And while motivations and influences can affect our core opinions, these core opinions still reign supreme as the ultimate measure of forward action. As is the case with the other outer drivers, the opinions dynamic is heavily influenced by each of the other inner drivers, outer qualities, and the reciprocal connectivity that exists naturally in the CIBIC system.

MOTIVATIONS (AN INTERACTIVE QUALITY)

The third outer quality of Motivations, as described by the prevailing obligations, responsibilities, accountabilities, and commitments that exist, highlights your ability to individually or collectively meet motivation-driven expectations that exist with family members, peers, clients, and other interests. Motivations highlight your ability to leverage, promote, and otherwise use obligations, responsibilities, accountabilities, commitments, joy, love, happiness, desire, drive, and pride among others to facilitate, enable, or limit the pursuit of a desired outcome or end goal. For singular and collective interests, these noneconomic motivators can significantly influence general decision making at a fundamental level, acting as a wild card in the unpredictable influence and control decision making and actions realm. As is the case with the other outer drivers, the motivations dynamic is heavily influenced by each of the other inner drivers, outer qualities, and the reciprocal connectivity that exists naturally in the CIBIC system.

PROFICIENCY (A PERFORMANCE QUALITY)

The fourth outer quality of Proficiencies, as described by the prevailing precision, efficiency, creativity, and familiarity expectations that exist, highlights your ability to individually or collectively meet proficiency-driven expectations that exist with family members, peers, clients, and other interests. Proficiency highlights the dynamic pursuit of perfection, accuracy, precision, quality, and excellence as a success-promoting endeavor. Be it through the utilization of skill sets, cognitive tools, proficiency resources, or best practices, the pursuit of proficiency is both essential and critical to the pursuit of excellence. While knowledge acquisition, skill set development, Lean practices, and process awareness can fuel this pursuit, only your commitment to excellence can truly promote your success in this endeavor. And while some may value quantity (output) over quality, true proficiency enthusiasts recognize that quantity without quality is wasteful, meaningless, and unproductive. For individual and collective interests, there is simply no substitute for accuracy, precision, quality, and the pursuit of excellence. While proficiency promotes excellence, incompetence promotes mediocrity and failure. As such, your willingness to embrace proficiency can and often will have far-reaching implications to your pursuit of excellence. As is the case with the other outer drivers, the proficiencies dynamic is heavily influenced by each of the other inner drivers, outer qualities, and the reciprocal connectivity that exists naturally in the CIBIC system.

OUTPUT (A PERFORMANCE QUALITY)

The fifth outer quality of Output, as described by your production, volume, capacity, and yield dynamics, highlights your ability to individually or collectively meet output-driven expectations that exist with family members, peers, clients, and other interests. Output highlights your ability to produce work, effort, volume, energy, and power. Be it through physical exertion or mental effort, the creation of output promotes the creation of value through tangible effort. For individual and collective interests, the ability and willingness to produce work, effort, volume, energy, and power are often a key determinant of perceived performance. In many instances, that perceived performance determines trade, professional, or academic good standing or lack thereof. For virtually all interests, that good standing or lack thereof directly influences the performance-driven pursuit of continuous improvement and sustainability. While your output or lack thereof is usually classified in terms of actual work, effort, volume, energy, and power, on occasion, it is classified in terms of mass available capacity or production potential.

As is the case with the other outer drivers, the output dynamic is heavily influenced by each of the other inner drivers, outer qualities, and the reciprocal connectivity that exists naturally in the CIBIC system.

SUSTAINABILITY (A PERFORMANCE QUALITY)

The sixth outer quality of Sustainability, as described by your continuity, perpetuity, regularity, and conservation, highlights your ability to individually or collectively meet sustainability expectations that exist with family members, peers, clients, and other interests. Sustainability highlights your ability to promote or continue an activity, pursuit, action, or endeavor ad infinitum. Powered by your discipline, desire, resilience, and a strong will, sustainability is critical to your pursuit of excellence and continuous improvement at all levels. As both an inner driver and an outer quality, as designed, sustainability is the most important element of the CIBIC system. Without sustainability, there is no continuity, and vice versa. And although intermittent, short-term, sporadic, and irregular performance standards may appeal to some, the true pursuit of excellence is only possible through sustainability, continuity, and perpetuity. As is the case with the other outer drivers, the sustainability dynamic is heavily influenced by each of the other inner drivers, outer qualities, and the reciprocal connectivity that exists naturally in the CIBIC system.

INFLUENCES (AN INTERACTIVE QUALITY)

The seventh outer quality of Influences, as described by your networks, affiliations, collaborations, and relationships, highlights your ability to individually or collectively meet the influence-driven expectations that exist with family members, peers, clients, and other interests. Influences highlight the power and influence of networking, affiliation, collaboration, and relationships in the qualities and expectations endeavor. For individual and collective interests, the ability and willingness to affiliate, network, collaborate, and team with others are an essential requirement for those who desire to succeed. Networks, associations, cartels, committees, teams, and interest groups can each influence the expectations dynamic in ways that can and often will influence your chosen pursuits. While some discount the power of influence, the truly wise come to understand that sometimes "it's not what you know, it's who you know" that determines your long-term success. Be it through social, brokered, organized, or leveraged relationships, your ability to control your outcome often hangs in the balance of this quality. As is the case with the other outer drivers, the influences dynamic is heavily influenced by each of the other inner drivers, outer qualities, and the reciprocal connectivity that exists naturally in the CIBIC system.

TIMELINESS (A BENEFIT QUALITY)

The eighth outer quality of Timeliness, as described by your reliability, punctuality, earliness, and speediness, highlights your ability to individually or collectively meet the time-driven expectations of family members, peers, clients, and other interests. Timeliness highlights your ability to be timely, reliable, speedy, or early in your chosen pursuits. For singular and collective interests, your ability to achieve, embrace, and promote punctuality will ultimately promote your time-specific viability and credibility. While timeliness will open the door of opportunity, tardiness will often slam the door shut. From chronological, cycle, lead, delivery, schedule, arrival, departure, work, trip, and pickup times, to deadline dates, the importance of time is undeniable. Those who master the nuances of timeliness will be uniquely qualified to pursue excellence in this endeavor. As is the case with the other outer drivers, the timeliness dynamic is heavily influenced by each of the other inner drivers, outer qualities, and the reciprocal connectivity that exists naturally in the CIBIC system.

ECONOMICS (A BENEFIT QUALITY)

The ninth outer quality of Economics, as described by the prevailing compensation, cost, price, and value dynamics that exist, highlights your ability to individually or collectively meet the economic expectations of family members, peers, clients, and other interests. Economics highlights your ability to create, develop, leverage, gain, or otherwise use money, assets, profit, gain, currency, value, compensation, and tangible exchange to limit or promote the pursuit and achievement of a desired outcome. For virtually all individual and collective interests, the ability and willingness to recognize price, cost, compensation, gain, and profit as the precursors of favorability, goodwill, high esteem, continued employment, and purchase affirmation are essential for success in an incredibly significant number of endeavors. To discount the value that the price and pay qualities have in modern societies is to discount the reality of how things really work in the modern world. As is the case with the other outer drivers, the economics dynamic is heavily influenced by each of the other inner drivers, outer qualities, and the reciprocal connectivity that exists naturally in the CIBIC system.

METRICS AND DYNAMICS

Your outer qualities influence your outer realities, plain and simple. Individual and collective interests with strong inner drivers and outer qualities almost always experience success at much higher levels than their peers. And those same interests who embrace the nuances of the CIBIC system enjoy success at even greater levels. Their ability to meet and exceed expectations through the recognition and use of the CIBIC frameworks, methods, and tools simultaneously promotes their pursuit of excellence and continuous improvement in a manner that is organized and efficient. While the development of your inner drivers was the first step in that pursuit, other steps are clearly needed to continue that pursuit. The second step in that pursuit is embracing the development of your inner drivers AND outer qualities as the essential precursor of excellence. While acknowledging the connection between your inner power and outer strength helps in this pursuit, only your full comprehension of inner driver and outer quality reciprocity can guarantee that pursuit. As we discussed earlier, the CIBIC Cognitive Dynamics Sphere is a visual model for highlighting the connection between the inner drivers and the outer qualities. In CIBIC, each inner driver influences each outer quality, and vice versa. When the strength of one inner driver wanes, the strength of the other inner drivers and outer qualities also wanes, highlighting the dynamic connections that exist between both. In nature, the most geometrically perfect way to highlight that dynamic connection is through the use of the CIBIC 18-Point Cognitive Dynamics Sphere. Although we highlighted the left hemisphere inner drivers earlier, we only gave fleeting attention to the right hemisphere outer qualities. The outer qualities right hemisphere Cognitive Dynamics Sphere is highlighted in Figure 4.2. Each of the nine outer qualities is arranged around the perimeter of the sphere

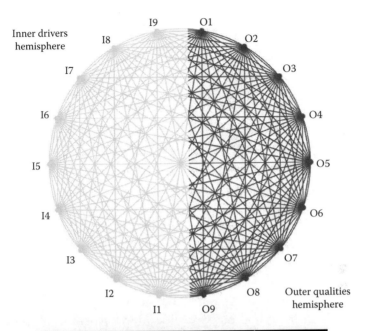

FIGURE 4.2
Cognitive Dynamics Sphere—outer qualities hemisphere.

Designation	Description	Designation	Description
I1	Stability	O1	Convenience
I2	Adaptability	O2	Opinions
I3	Planning	O3	Motivations
I4	Patience	O4	Proficiencies
I5	Humility	O5	Output
I6	Intelligence	O6	Sustainability
I7	Resilience	O7	Influences
I8	Enthusiasm	O8	Timeliness
I9	Sustainability	O9	Economics

to promote our substantive discussion of the cognitive sphere system, and to promote our later discussions of expectations and change management. While the pursuit of change should be your goal, seeking change and creating change are uniquely separate endeavors. While your outer strength can promote change, creating that outer strength is not without its challenges. In the presence of confusion, uncertainty, and misfortune, building your outer strength can become both improbable and unlikely. To be plagued by this confusion, uncertainty, and misfortune is sad, but to be plagued by this same confusion, uncertainty, and misfortune with no means of resolution is calamitous. British mathematician and historian

Jacob Bronowski once stated that "Knowledge is an unending adventure at the edge of uncertainty."

By developing your outer qualities, you help to vanquish confusion, uncertainty, and misfortune through your commitment and actions in support of that pursuit. Your ability to transform your inner power to your outer strength directly aids in that pursuit. In all of our endeavors, all of our practices, and all of our pursuits, embracing and leveraging the outer qualities have great profound importance. While the loss of opportunity is sad, the waste of potential can be utterly devastating. By developing your inner drivers and outer qualities, you help to eradicate the waste of potential that plagues far too many interests. By further embracing the Cognitive Dynamics Sphere to promote that development, you help to promote the value, achievement, preference, and performance that can fuel your pursuit of a better tomorrow. In the coming chapters, we will discuss the configuration, development, and change subject matters in a manner that embraces the Cognitive Dynamics Sphere as a driving promoter of inner driver and outer qualities development. Embracing this subject matter will go a long way toward helping you to pursue continuous improvement and excellence.

Courage Is the First of Human Qualities Because It Guarantees the Others.

ARISTOTLE

Nothing Endures but Personal Qualities.

WALT WHITMAN

5

Configuration

There is one looming question that we each must answer. Do you develop then configure or configure then develop? Do we decide and then make it happen, or make it happen and then decide? While strategists prefer to configure and then develop, tacticians prefer to develop and then configure. In CIBIC, configuration always precedes development, unless chosen otherwise for specific reasons. Referred to as customization by some, personalization by others, and transformation by the chosen few, the science, art, and practice of configuration have no equal. The power to tweak, revise, reshape, adjust, and reform helps to shape the human dynamic in ways that most fail to recognize. Adaptable people, computer devices, custom machinery, smart telephones, and many cutting-edge modern devices are each able to morph based on current conditions. In human-factors continuous improvement, fewer endeavors are more critical than the endeavor of learning how to use or exploit what we have, own, or otherwise possess to promote the pursuit of a specific goal. This science, practice, and art, which is commonly referred to as configuration, highlights the need for customization as a critical driver of excellence. Planned customization rises from your ability to recognize your prevailing **expectations** and **objectives** and then using that insight to focus and develop your outer **attributes** to address the prevailing challenges and opportunities that exist. While this pursuit may seem easy, it is generally anything but easy. The dynamic nature of your expectations, objectives, outer qualities, and chaotic realities makes the science, practice, and art of configuration a perpetually challenging endeavor. And while CIBIC makes this a much easier pursuit, your success in this endeavor will still require painstaking effort and continual analysis. Just consider the expectation dynamic for starters. In CIBIC, your expectation realities fall into one of three categories; expectation deficit, expectation balance, and expectation surplus.

The first category, expectations **deficit**, highlights instances in which current capabilities fall short of current expectations. While sometimes a stressful category to endure, the expectations deficit category highlights the need for corrective action as the precursor of excellence and continuous improvement. The second category, expectations **balance**, highlights instances in which current capabilities meet current expectations. This category is synonymous with the adequate level of performance and quality that perpetuates your chosen endeavors. The third and final category, expectations **surplus**, highlights instances in which current capabilities exceed current expectations. This category is synonymous with the superior level of performance and quality that promotes best-in-class status and recognition. Your recognition and comprehension of the expectation categories promote the comprehensive expectations management that promotes your pursuit of excellence. Regardless of the specific categories that exist, your challenge, plain and simple, is to continually develop, sequence, and deploy (configure) your attributes and qualities to address these expectation realities. Just as changing expectations can drive configuration, changing objectives can also drive configuration in the same way. Every endeavor, pursuit, and venture challenges us in different ways. Some of these endeavors, pursuits, and ventures require sustainability and others require the capacity to produce at a high level. Some endeavors, pursuits, and ventures require strength in one area while others require strength in multiple areas. As your endeavors, pursuits, and ventures change, so do your configuration dynamics. While your inner drivers, collective attributes, outer qualities, and core competencies are your available resources for achieving excellence, only the proper configuration of these resources can guarantee that excellence. While the masses meander through life, clueless about the importance of configuration, CIBIC enthusiasts and CIBIC practitioners learn to leverage their inner drivers, collective attributes, outer qualities, and core competencies to power the pursuit of excellence and continuous improvement. At a practical level, this pursuit begins with active gap management and elimination. As we mentioned earlier, gaps highlight the difference between our current realities and our desired realities, a reality in which our capabilities always exceed the prevailing expectations. In most cases, the resolution of gaps is neither magical nor mystical. In specific terms, gap resolution is only possible through the measured leveraging of inner drivers, collective attributes, outer qualities, and core competencies. In CIBIC, that measured leveraging is a natural product of configuration and staging as highlighted in the EDGE framework. By sequencing and staging the required inner drivers, collective attributes, outer qualities, and core competencies, the configuration phase refines and enhances the development activities that are critical to your pursuits. Rather than addressing deficiencies and deficits haphazardly and spontaneously, active configuration promotes continuous improvement that is both organized and systemic. By mastering the nuances of configuration, you promote the pursuit of excellence in a manner that is repeatable and adoptable, thus promoting continuous improvement at both the individual and collective levels. While a single expectation can provoke good discussion, only the itemization of multiple expectations can truly promote successful configuration. The CIBIC Required Expectations Summary (REX) provides a model for driving this configuration pursuit. By itemizing expectations, capabilities, attribute relevance, and development needs, the REX promotes the efficient structure and effective standardization that promotes your configuration endeavors.

This same linear process of configuration can be visualized using the Cognitive Dynamics Sphere, as shown in Figure 5.1. The right hemisphere, the outer qualities zone of the Cognitive Dynamics Sphere, highlights individual and collective attributes that address our outer realities. The left hemisphere, the inner drivers zone of the Cognitive Dynamics Sphere, highlights individual and collective attributes that reflect our inner realities. While the inner expectations have unique importance, it is the outer expectations that influence our ability to achieve excellence as determined by the outside world. Once you understand the nuances of configuration and the expectations dynamic, you will be generally prepared to develop your qualities, competencies, and capabilities to achieve your stated end goal. This development will later support your downstream deployment, and continuation activities that will further support your pursuit of excellence. By helping you to identify and manage the various nuances of configuration, the CIBIC system, EDGE, and the REX help to promote the resolution, elimination, and management of gaps in a manner that promotes the full pursuit of excellence. While continuous improvement is about exceeding expectations, that pursuit is anything but easy. The chaotic and ever-changing nature of our existence makes expectations management a truly dynamic endeavor, full of challenges. By embracing CIBIC and the CIBIC system, the process of configuration, as a precursor of excellence, becomes a much easier endeavor.

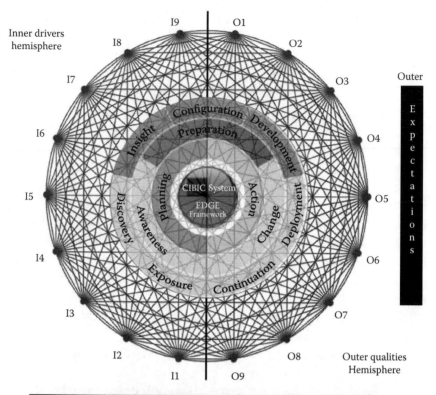

Designation	Description	Designation	Description
I1	Stability	O1	Convenience
I2	Adaptability	O2	Opinions
I3	Planning	O3	Motivations
I4	Patience	O4	Proficiencies
I5	Humility	O5	Output
I6	Intelligence	O6	Sustainability
I7	Resilience	O7	Influences
I8	Enthusiasm	O8	Timeliness
I9	Sustainability	O9	Economics

FIGURE 5.1

The dynamics of configuration.

Perfect Configuration Almost
Always Promotes Perfect
Results.

MICHAEL DAVIS

When We Reconfigure
Ourselves, We Redefine Who
We Are.

F. ALLEN DAVIS

6

The Dynamics of Development

While the importance of configuration is critical and undeniable, it pales in importance to the downstream importance of development. In Chapter 5, we pondered the question, do you develop and then configure or configure and then develop? As was the case in Chapter 5, there is a second burning question that looms over this subject matter. Do you develop and then deploy or deploy and then develop? Build and then act or act and then build? While strategists prefer to develop before they deploy, tacticians often choose to deploy before they develop. In CIBIC, development always precedes deployment, unless special conditions exist. By embracing development as the precursor of deployment, we promote the orderly pursuit of excellence. While development is the practice of evolving, acquiring, growing, refining, and maturing to promote the pursuit of a chosen objective, deployment is the direct action, motion, and movement that create the desired change. As the direct precursor of deployment, development promotes the pursuit of our chosen objectives through direct **acquisition and refinement**. In the truest sense, it is only through development that continuous improvement and excellence can prevail, thrive, and endure. In the absence of development, our dreams for a better tomorrow wane, the victim of inadequacy and ineptitude. Development is the practice, art, or endeavor of enhancing our acumen, skill sets, capabilities, and resources through the before-mentioned acquisition and refinement. While some classify development only in terms of formal education, such a classification is faulty at best. Your formal education only represents a small percentage of your developmental endeavors. The remaining elements of your development rise from the haze of the undefined and misunderstood. While some of us require a formal education to develop, others require refinement and special finishing to more efficiently and effectively utilize what we already possess. As a general rule, we are each faced with different realities that influence the development endeavor. Some of us face educational deficits, some of us face social deficits, some of us face experience deficits, and yet others face exposure deficits that greatly influence the development dynamic. While some approach their developmental challenges haphazardly, CIBIC promotes the use of the EDGE-driven systemic approach to development that highlights the use of structure, visualization, acronymization, and intonation to promote the development of our critical attributes. By standardizing development system and methods, CIBIC elevates the endeavor of development to a new level of efficiency. By specifically emphasizing the use of visualization and acronymization, CIBIC makes complex subject matters easier to comprehend and retain. This development approach was specifically designed to make subject matters like the inner drivers, outer qualities, EDGE framework, cognitive awareness, and chaos much easier to comprehend and significantly easier to retain. At the heart of the CIBIC development system is the comprehensively elegant EDGE framework. The EDGE framework is designed to promote the before-mentioned acquisition and refinement that are key elements of the development process. Before you can understand the entire development process, you must first understand the specific nuances of development beginning with acquisition and refinement. **Acquisition** is the process of acquiring new skill sets, resources, and capabilities that are designed to promote the pursuit of designated goals and objectives. **Refinement**, on the other hand, is the process of refining, evolving, cultivating, or focusing existing skill sets, resources, and capabilities to promote the pursuit of designated goals and objectives. This acquisition and refinement tandem form the foundation of the development complex. As was the case with configuration, a better understanding of development is possible through the Cognitive Dynamics Sphere visualization. As a critical endeavor, the development of both your inner drivers and outer qualities is essential to your pursuit of excellence. In the Cognitive Dynamics Sphere visual shown in Figure 6.1, the inner drivers and outer qualities are shown with the EDGE framework visually superimposed for effect. As is the case with the previous Cognitive Dynamic Sphere visuals, the inner drivers are shown in the left hemisphere while the outer qualities are shown in the right hemisphere. As was the case earlier, the same degree of reciprocity between the inner drivers and outer qualities continues to exist. In your inner and outer development endeavors, the inner drivers and outer qualities are each developed through the acquisition or refinement appropriate for your chosen endeavor. In endeavors where time sensitivity

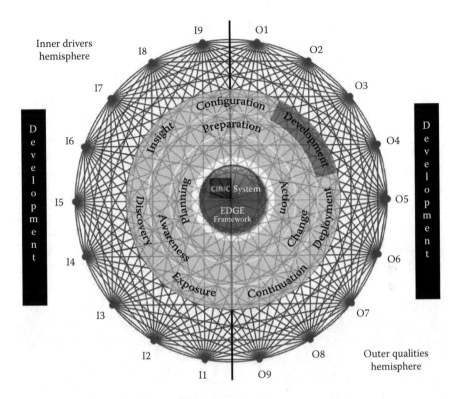

Inner drivers hemisphere

Outer qualities hemisphere

Development system

Promote performance, learning, resource, and reality management excellence and continuous improvement through the use of EDGE framework awareness and preparation dynamics in concert with CIBIC system retention tools.

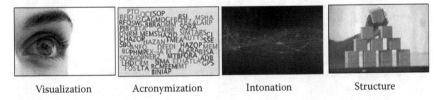

| Visualization | Acronymization | Intonation | Structure |

FIGURE 6.1
The EDGE framework and development.

is critical, the development of your outer qualities timeliness attribute may be necessary, and in other instances, the development of other outer qualities may be necessary. Correspondingly, in endeavors where the level of precision is critical, the development of your outer qualities' proficiencies attribute may be necessary. The same dynamic applies to the development of your inner drivers. In endeavors where proficiency is critical, high levels of intelligence are needed to promote this pursuit. In endeavors where timeliness is critical, high levels of planning and adaptability will likely be needed to promote this pursuit. While most development systems tend to be dull, boring, and lackluster, CIBIC embraces visualization, acronymization, intonation, and structure to promote, accelerate, and perpetuate the development process. The development system subject matter is specifically designed to extend its application and use far beyond the limited use time frames that we typically see in real-world scenarios.

Although the combined use of visualization, acronymization, intonation, and structure in the CIBIC system may be novel, their individual use has spanned thousands of years. From learning our ABC's and how to spell Mississippi by song and poem, to learning to use I before E except after C, the creative use of visualization, acronymization, intonation, and structure can be seen everywhere we look. As an engineering student, I learned to remember the color code of a resistor by memorizing a story about a girl named Violet. As a graduate student, I condensed the entire accounting methodology into a two-word phrase that allowed me to quickly master basic accounting principles. Others have used visualization, acronymization, intonation, and structure for retention without even knowing it. Isn't it ironic how individuals who can't memorize basic concepts one moment can be seen singing the words of a song with perfect pitch and harmony the next, not knowing why they can accomplish such a feat. The use of intonation extends far beyond the use of song to promote retention. Some tribes in Africa have used intonation in the form of poetry and song for thousands of years to capture and retain their comprehensive tribal history. Despite its power in the realm of development, the use of structure, visualization, acronymization, and intonation is sadly the exception and not the rule. And while some have the natural ability to capture, manage, and retain large amounts of information, most simply lack this ability. Limited mental bandwidth and the limited capacity to retain concepts and principles provide significant developmental challenges for most people. By using SAPPHIRES, COMPOSITE, EDGE, FACET, and some of the other acronymization tools as retention concepts, CIBIC bridges the limited bandwidth gap in a manner that is both effective and efficient. And while CIBIC does not dictate your use of skill-specific learning tools, it does encourage you to embrace retention as a key element of your skill building endeavors. While most development systems only highlight very basic development system attributes, CIBIC goes a step further. By highlighting key system attributes that solidify and reinforce the longer-term retention of key development concepts, CIBIC promotes the pursuit and excellence and continuous improvement in a new and exciting way. The visualization elements are designed to convey the dynamics of CIBIC using illustrations that promote comprehension and retention. The acronymization elements are designed to promote the retention of key process-specific concepts. The intonation elements, although not widely used, are designed to promote the retention of high-content subject matters. And, the structure elements are designed to promote the organized and systemic use of the CIBIC subject matter. Together, these four developmental dynamics highlight and promote the efficient use and application of CIBIC and any other subject matter that you choose to embrace. Once you master the nuances of configuration and development, change will appear right over the horizon.

The Growth and Development of People Is the Highest Calling of Leadership.

HARVEY FIRESTONE

Growth Is the Evidence of Life.

JOHN HENRY NEWMAN

7

The Dynamics of Change

All of your power, all of your resources, and all of your newly found insight mean nothing if you can't leverage these attributes to create change. In order to change, you must first understand change and then embark on a path of definitive action to create the change that you desire. Change is the manifestation of three dynamics: **motion**, **intent**, and **guidance** (MIG). Motion is the creation of change through your definitive actions or lack thereof. Intent highlights the specific goals and objectives that drive your pursuit of change. Guidance, on the other hand, highlights the qualifiers that refine the dynamics of your change-driven pursuits. While your superficial understanding of these three dynamics will aid you in the pursuit of change, only your comprehensive understanding of these three dynamics, beginning with motion, will truly promote your pursuit of excellence. Although some think of motion as a singular phenomenon, nothing could be further from the truth. Motion, as a change-promoting dynamic, is the manifestation of five action-based dynamics: coordination, resolution, elimination, acquisition, and management. **Coordination** is the endeavor or practice of directly sequencing, allocating, or ordering tangible or intangible resources to promote the pursuit of a chosen deliverable. As we saw in earlier chapters, in the CIBIC system, coordination represents the alignment and sequencing of your inner drivers and outer qualities to promote a desired outcome. **Resolution** is the endeavor of proactively resolving a change-promoting or -preventing problem or situation by emphasizing gap responsibility, accountability, solvability, and preventability as a fundamental pursuit. The resolution process can easily be remembered using the GRASP (gap responsibility, accountability, solvability, and preventability) acronym. **Elimination** is the endeavor or practice of directly acting to eliminate all change-preventing impediments. As opposed to the other change elements, elimination exclusively focuses on the negation of an impediment. Elimination represents the direct effort or physical action focused toward the desired change as mandated during the planning and alignment endeavor. **Acquisition** is the endeavor or practice of acquiring new tangible and intangible resources that promote the pursuit of excellence and continuous improvement. While in the financial world, acquisition might highlight a business or asset acquisition, in the academic world, acquisition might highlight the acquisition of new knowledge or an academic degree. **Management** is the endeavor or practice of directing or overseeing specific activities that promote the pursuit of excellence and continuous improvement. The management element focuses on the non-action-based supervisory participation in your change endeavors. Together, these five change dynamics create the motion required to create change. The second change-promoting dynamic, **intent**, is just as complex and just as important. Although some think of intent as a singularly simple phenomenon, nothing could be further from the truth. Intent, as a change-promoting dynamic, is the real-world manifestation of your mission, objective, strategy, and tactic-driven pursuit of change. Before we can create change, we must first know what kind of change we are trying to create. When we covered the chaos, gap, and planning subject matters earlier, the intent was to help you build the general skill sets designed to promote your competency in this pursuit. The CIBIC Professional Tools Library was additionally designed to help you improve your plan-specific competencies to aid you in the pursuit of change. The third change-promoting dynamic, **guidance**, presents a unique set of challenges and considerations. Guidance, as a change-promoting dynamic, is the real-world manifestation of the focus, approach, commitment, expectation, and timing-driven considerations of change, hereafter referred to as the **five facets of change**. The five facets of change are visually highlighted in Figure 7.1. The **Focus** facet relates to your planned decision to pursue change as an individual and/or collective endeavor, focusing on the use of either some or all of the inner drivers and outer qualities. Focus is designed to refine your change-driven pursuits to pursuits that are deemed necessary and essential. The **Approach** facet relates to your planned decision to pursue change either progressively as a planned forward pursuit or regressively as a planned "working backward" pursuit. The Approach facet heavily relies on the use of the EDGE framework as the planned sequence model for all change-based pursuits. The **Commitment** facet relates to your planned decision to embrace the pursuit of change as either a Paradigm A (Undercommit–Overperform) or Paradigm Z

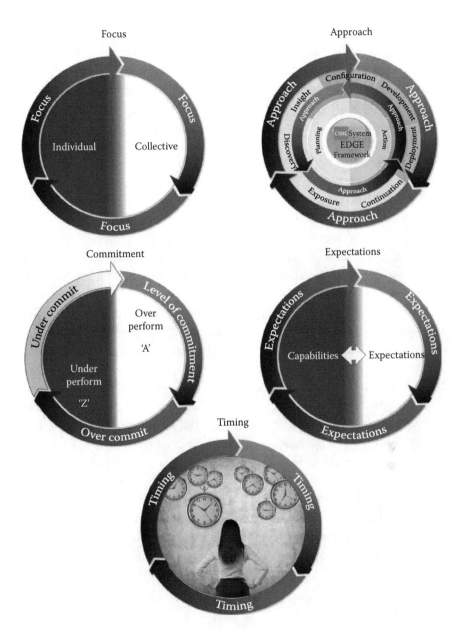

FIGURE 7.1
The five facets of change.

(Overcommit–Underperform) pursuit as illustrated in the Tom Powers' Theory of Expectations model.[3] Although the CIBIC system embraces the Paradigm A model, it is nonetheless important for you to acknowledge the great level of influence that the commitment facet can have on the general pursuit of change. The **Expectations** facet relates to the expectation management subject matter as it relates to your capability and expectation dynamics. The delicate balance between your current capabilities and your current expectations holds great importance to your change-driven pursuits. Although the CIBIC system embraces meeting or exceeding prevailing expectations as the essential precursor of excellence, it is nonetheless important for you to understand the great level of importance that the expectations facet can have on the general pursuit of change. The fifth and final facet of change is the timing element. The **Timing** facet relates to the time relative subject matter as it relates to the time dynamics of your change-driven endeavors.

The timing facet acknowledges the **immediate**, **near-term**, and **longer-term** timing considerations that exist in your change-related endeavors, acknowledging the great fundamental role that this timing dynamic plays in the pursuit of change. These five guidance-specific change facets highlight the generally cognitive dynamics that influence the pursuit of change. As is the case with the general CIBIC subject matter, the development and retention concept embraced earlier in this book are also embraced in the change narrative to promote proficiency and efficiency. In the motion dynamic, the coordination, resolution, elimination, acquisition, and management dynamics are represented using the **CREAM** acronym while the guidance dynamic focus, approach, commitment, expectations, and timing dynamics are represented using the **FACET** acronym. Now that you have new awareness of the motion, intent, and guidance dynamics of change, we can now discuss the change participant subject matter.

THE CHANGE PARTICIPANTS

While your newly discovered motion, intent, and guidance will promote your pursuit of change, that pursuit is incomplete without a full understanding of the dynamics of change participation. Change seldom if ever occurs in a vacuum, the manifestation of a single inhabitant world. Change is almost always the manifestation of very dynamic interpersonal considerations that must be considered and reconciled. When we discussed the five motion dynamics earlier, the discussion of coordination, resolution, elimination, acquisition, and management was pursued without expanding on the breadth and depth of participants in these endeavors. Recognizing these change participants or agents for change, as highlighted in Figure 7.2, is essential for the pursuit of change. Although change is often viewed as a single participant endeavor, that is almost never the case. Even in your singular pursuits, the involvement of other people, other groups, and other organizations in the pursuit of change is undeniable and unquestionable. Your challenge is learning to identify the different "agents for change" that exist for you individually and collectively. Although there are an almost endless number of change agent types, four types are more widely observed than the others: the Buyers and Sellers, the Managers, the Producers, and the Marketers, as shown in Figure 7.2. The **Buyers and Sellers**, also referred to as the "Winders," are the individual or collective interests that buy or sell goods, services, resources, and other tangible or intangible items. These individuals and collective interests often create or promote the actual stimulus for change that exists.

The **Managers**, also referred to as the "Minders," are those individuals or collective interests who direct, oversee, or drive the actual pursuit of continuous improvement and excellence at a high level. These individuals and collective interests often stipulate the need for change, and often oversee endeavors to create the required change. These Managers include but are not limited to the C-Suite, Presidential, Director, Managerial, and senior-level individual and collective interests who participate in the change endeavor at a very high level. The **Producers**, also referred to as the "Grinders," are the individual and collective interests who are directly accountable for producing the required change elements at a basic level. These are the individuals, teams, and collective interests who are directly responsible for producing the products, services, or desired end results that are gauged against change-driven expectations. The **Marketers**, also referred to as the "Finders," are primarily those individuals and collective interests responsible for promoting, merchandising, or advocating the change-driven product, services, or desired end result. Each of the four agents for change plays a vastly different role in the pursuit of change. While Buyers and Sellers play a major role in the motion-driven acquisition dynamic, they play a much smaller role in the coordination, resolution, execution, and management dynamics. Producers, on the other

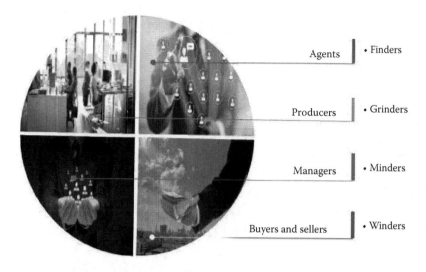

Agents | • Finders

Producers | • Grinders

Managers | • Minders

Buyers and sellers | • Winders

Agents	Producers	Managers	Buyers/sellers
Distributors	Skilled labor	Presidents	Consumers
Representatives	Unskilled labor	Executives	Suppliers
Marketers	Technicians	Directors	Clients
Advocates	Administrators	Managers	Contributors
Lobbyist	Educators	Parents	Constituents
Diplomats	Professionals	Principals	
Merchandiser		Superintendent	

FIGURE 7.2

The change participants.

hand, play a major role in the motion-driven resolution and execution dynamics and a lesser role in the coordination, acquisition, and management dynamics. The Markers and Managers also play uniquely different roles in the pursuit of change as mandated by the specific circumstances that exist. As a CIBIC practitioner, it is important that you continually evaluate your environment to identify and highlight the specific realities that influence the change participant dynamic. By collectively recognizing the motion, intent, and guidance dynamics of change and the role of the change participants, you help to make the pursuit of change a much easier endeavor to manage and control.

CHANGE-PROMOTING TOOLS

As an "upstream" continuous improvement system, CIBIC can help you to promote the change that you seek. Without the CIBIC Professional Tools Library, the pursuit of change becomes a much more difficult endeavor. The CIBIC Professional Tools Library includes a full array of CIBIC guides, worksheets, and surveys that promote the use of CIBIC in your everyday endeavors. This library includes the Inner Driver Survey (IDS) that is used to assess inner driver strength, the Peer Review Survey (IDR) that is used to validate inner driver dynamics, the Master Worksheet that is used to organize and segment all key analytics, the Required Expectations Summary (REX) that is used to itemize prevailing expectations and your ability to meet those expectations, the Change Initiating Procedure (CHIP) that is designed to highlight the dynamics of the required changes needed to promote your chosen goals, the Chaos and Gap Elimination (CAGE) Worksheet that is designed to help you itemize the prevailing gaps and chaotic factors that exist, the Drivers and Qualities Maximization Worksheet (MAX) that promotes the focused itemization and development of your inner drivers and outer qualities, the subfactor development worksheet (SDW) that promotes the development of your critical subfactors, and the Mission and Objectives Summary Table (MOST) that is designed to help you identify your mission-specific gaps. Together, these professional tools help you to enthusiastically and effectively pursue continuous improvement, sustainability, excellence, and the change that promote all three. The pursuit of change is an endeavor that confuses some, confounds many, and challenges nearly everyone in one form or another. And while minimal change is generally common, optimal change is incredibly challenging to promote, create, and perpetuate without the right philosophy, framework, model, and system. In its optimal form, change eliminates chaos and gaps while also promoting the pursuit of excellence and continuous improvement. Although some may be driven to accept the status quo, when that status quo includes the presence of chaos, maintaining that status quo is simply not an acceptable alternative. Only through CIBIC can you identify and pursue the change that promotes a better tomorrow for yourself and others. For those who are strong, focused, committed, and willing, the pursuit of excellence and continuous improvement will always remain well within reach.

CREATING CHANGE (DEPLOYMENT AND MOTION)

As we stated earlier, change and the creation of motion are only possible through the coordination, resolution, elimination, acquisition, and management of your change-promoting endeavors. Once you embrace this reality, the change that you seek becomes much easier to create and perpetuate. But in the final analysis, only your willingness to become a true agent for change will promote the change you seek. Change is the manifestation of your desire to reject the status quo as allowable and acceptable. When we continue the same old practices, the same old routine, and the same old insanities, change can never prosper. Change requires courage, vision, discipline, and commitment; courage to face the challenges that change creates; the vision to anticipate the chaos that looms in the distance; and the discipline to stay on the right path when shortcuts will tempt you otherwise. While the CIBIC Professional Tools Library can aid you in the pursuit of change, only your cognitive awareness of change will help you to guarantee those pursuits. At a high level, our inner power promotes the outer strength that creates the change that we desire. By building our inner power, we build the outer strengths that in turn promote new competencies and capabilities. These new competencies and capabilities by default help to create the change that we seek. When we couple these competencies and capabilities with definitive action in pursuit of a goal or objective, change will always ensue. Recognizing and embracing the power of the CIBIC Cognitive Dynamics Sphere, as highlighted in Figure 7.3, is a good first step toward promoting change. As we discussed

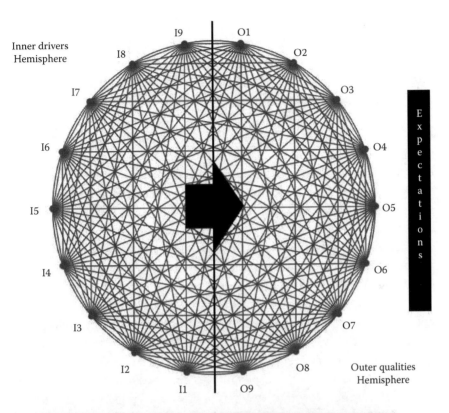

Designation	Description	Designation	Description
I1	Stability	O1	Convenience
I2	Adaptability	O2	Opinions
I3	Planning	O3	Motivations
I4	Patience	O4	Proficiencies
I5	Humility	O5	Output
I6	Intelligence	O6	Sustainability
I7	Resilience	O7	Influences
I8	Enthusiasm	O8	Timeliness
I9	Sustainability	O9	Economics

FIGURE 7.3
Change and the Cognitive Dynamics Sphere.

earlier, your inner drivers and outer qualities are elegantly interconnected and interdependent. Our inner drivers promote the outer qualities that are gauged against the prevailing expectations for change. When those outer qualities exceed the expectations for change, then change will likely occur. However, when the outer qualities fail to meet the same expectations for change, then change is unlikely. Although some may think of change as existing in a vacuum, that is seldom the case. Change is almost always the manifestation of our direct actions to promote change as influenced and driven by the five facets of change that we discussed earlier. Without question, the focus, approach, commitment, expectations, and timing dynamics influence, control, and promote the pursuit of change individually and collectively.

When we recognize this reality, we help to promote the change that we seek. The CIBIC system is designed to promote change, motion, and deployment through greater awareness, active engagement, and the tireless pursuit of stated goals and objectives. When we embrace CIBIC, our ability to promote change increases, the product of the improved proficiencies that the system promotes. And while our expectations and the expectations of others can influence our pursuit of change, there is no discounting the benefits and advantages that positive progress toward change can bring. Now that you have a greater awareness of the change dynamics, only your resistance to change can preclude your pursuit of excellence and continuous improvement. By continually embracing the CIBIC Professional Tools Library (PTL), you will greatly promote your pursuit of change and the benefits thereof.

You Must Be the Change You
Wish to See in the World.

MAHATMA GHANDI

Everyone Thinks of Changing
the World, but No One Thinks
of Changing Himself.

LEO TOLSTOY

8

New Perspectives

While comprehending that the CIBIC system is important, building a new awareness of continuous improvement is even more important. During our voyage of discovery, we covered a wide range of topics designed to highlight the critical elements that promote the pursuit of excellence and continuous improvement. Although this subject matter was designed to highlight the systemic elements of continuous improvement, it was also designed to help you build an improved intuitive comprehension of this subject matter. While system structure can help you to develop a consistent approach, it is only through the development of this intuitive comprehension that the entire pursuit of continuous improvement truly comes into focus. It is not good enough for you to understand how to manage a process; you should intuitively understand the purpose of the process in very fundamental terms. At the fundamental level, the CIBIC system is designed to promote the pursuit of continuous improvement as driven by three laws and five philosophies as highlighted in Figure 8.1 and described below. The three laws highlight the prevailing requirements that apply to this chosen pursuit. **The first law is that the pursuit of excellence and continuous improvement must be balanced, precise, tireless, and preemptive.** If you improve in a non-excellence-promoting fashion, then that improvement may not meet or exceed your expectations or the expectations of others, thus rendering your pursuit potentially unsuccessful. On the contrary, if you achieve short-term excellence that is not sustainable, then you once again may not meet or exceed prevailing expectations. As such, your failure to meet the first law can and most likely will limit your pursuit of excellence and continuous improvement.

The second law is that for every gap that exists, a negating inner driver or outer quality must exist and must be applied. The basic pursuit of continuous improvement is only possible if you have the means to

3 Laws	1	The pursuit of excellence and continuous improvement must be balanced, precise, tireless, and pre-emptive.
	2	For every gap, a negating driver or quality must exist and be applied.
	3	*Accepting* what's right, *respecting* what's right, and *embracing* what's right must drive your existence.

5 Philosophies	1	"Above All, Do No Harm to Yourself and Other." *Primum Non Nocere*
	2	"Never Lose Hope." *Nequaquam Depperamus*
	3	"Let the Doer Beware." *Caveat Actor*
	4	"Be Mindful of Your Surroundings." *Exsisto Memor of Vestri Amplexus*
	5	"Succeed from the Inside Out." *AB Intus Enim De Succedant*

FIGURE 8.1
The laws and philosophies.

counteract, eliminate, or resolve any, and all gaps, deficiencies, and chaotic factors that exist at the beginning of that pursuit.

The third law is that accepting what's right, respecting what's right, and embracing what's right must drive your existence. When we pursue a course of action based on our limited and sometimes biased self-interest rather than the collective best interest, catastrophes happen, sooner or later. However, albeit difficult sometimes, accepting, respecting, and embracing the truth and righteousness can often be the key to your salvation, now and later. Your ability to embrace and promote these three laws will undoubtedly promote the pursuit of excellence and continuous improvement that you seek. We have it in our power to achieve great things if we commit ourselves to doing so. The three laws can help you to achieve what you seek to achieve, if you are tirelessly committed to their use.

While the three laws can help to regulate your pursuit of excellence and continuous improvement, the five philosophies provide you with the philosophical frame of reference that can enhance and refine your pursuit. The five philosophies highlight the five intuitive considerations that refine and enhance each of the three laws. While simply listing these five philosophies would be easier for you to grasp, the inclusion of the Latin derivations for these five philosophies is included to highlight their significant fundamental importance. The first philosophy, *Primum non nocere*, is a Latin phrase that means **"Above all, do no harm."** Written in the fifth century BC, the Hippocratic Oath, which governs the behavior of physicians, is the oath pledged by physicians before they start to practice medicine. In societal terms, it is almost a certainty that the world would be a better place if we all followed this oath by limiting our harm to others. The second philosophy, *Nequaquam desperamus*, is a Latin phrase that means **"Never lose hope."** Through the course of your life, you will inevitably be faced with a variety of challenges that will test your strength of character and resolve. Some of these challenges will be demoralizing while others may be stressful to endure. In the face of our challenges, we must never yield to our fear and lose hope. Hope is always the precursor of new possibilities. The third philosophy, *Caveat Actor*, is a Latin phrase that means **"Let the doer beware."** All too often in the modern world, people rush to action and then cower in agony when those actions have catastrophic consequences. In many instances, those actions take place in the vacuum of idle-mindedness that occurs when people shun the art of advanced planning. The fourth philosophy, *Exsisto Memor Of Vestri Amplexus*, is a Latin phrase that means **"Be mindful of your surroundings."** We are all subject to and influenced by the realities of our surroundings, and when we fail to acknowledge or understand those realities, terrible things can happen. All of your strengths, weaknesses, opportunities, and threats are all tied to the realities of our surroundings. The fifth and final philosophy, *Ab Intus Enim De Succedant*, is a Latin phrase that means **"Succeed from the inside out."** The entire CIBIC system was developed to promote the development of your inner drivers and attributes as a necessary precursor of your outer development. When you choose to embrace the three laws, five philosophies, and the elegant dynamics of the CIBIC system, you promote the pursuit of a brighter future full of promise and full of opportunities. Make no mistake, my objective from page one of this book has been to help you decimate, eliminate, eradicate, extinguish, and vanquish the gaps, deficiencies, and chaotic realities that exist for you individually and collectively. While I acknowledge that some of these gaps, deficiencies, and chaotic realities are systemic, environmental, and generally beyond our control, the overwhelming reality is that most of these realities are the manifestation of our own decisions. Our tendencies to pursue fame, fortune, notoriety, acceptance, and recognition sometimes lead us to conduct ourselves in strangely unpredictable ways, embracing shortcuts and callous disregard as the preferred course of action. These actions are at the root of many of the societal dysfunctions that continue to plague modern society. CIBIC helps to address many of these problems through the use of a universally adaptable system that adheres to the generally intuitive principles of great thinkers from Albert Einstein to Sir Isaac Newton and from Voltaire to Aristotle. Although countless philosophers, authors, scholars, and theologians have attempted to address the pursuit of continuous improvement from a discipline-specific frame of reference, CIBIC attempts to address the continuous improvement subject matter in a manner that promotes universal applicability, acknowledging the distinct role that religion, science, philosophy, sociology, and academia play in the pursuit of continuous improvement. When you embrace CIBIC and its role in the endeavor of process, systems, and human capital continuous improvement, the future becomes brighter for yourself and others in your group, team, and organization. The only thing now standing in your way is your responsibility to act and promote the pursuit of excellence and continuous improvement.

Perfection Is Not Attainable, but If We Chase Perfection, We Can Catch Excellence.

VINCE LOMBARDI

Excellence Is Not an Exception, It's a Prevailing Attitude.

COLIN POWELL

9

Launching Your Pursuits

Individually, collectively, and organizationally, your new future begins today, not tomorrow, not next week, not next month, and not next year. As we discussed earlier, the world is a place where all our hopes, all our dreams, and all our desires are within the realm of the possible. Even the disenfranchised, handicapped, and scarred live in a world where anything is possible. Stephen Hawking, Hellen Keller, Stevie Wonder, and Jose Feliciano all rose from the limitations of their circumstances to achieve great things. Rather than dwelling on their hardships or drowning in their sorrows, they each focused on the task at hand, facing their challenges without hesitation or trepidation. We each have it in our power to rise above our challenges in the pursuit of excellence. Those who have the vision, and the commitment, and the courage will always be able to soar to the highest heights. Even amid the accelerating change and daunting challenges that we face today, the truly courageous among us continue to achieve what was previously impossible to achieve. From wounded warriors to refugees, new stories of courage are written every day. These courageous souls continue to rise above their limitations to achieve what was previously thought to be impossible. Your challenge is to rise to your true potential using the power of CIBIC and the power of the human spirit that we all possess. On this note, you have now concluded your voyage of discovery into the realm of CIBIC. By embracing CIBIC frameworks, models, and methods, you help yourself to pursue a better tomorrow full of the infinite potential for change. May this voyage of discovery inspire, empower, and drive you to reach your potential and ecceed your wildest expectations.

F. Allen Davis

Where There Is No Vision, There Is No Hope.

GEORGE WASHINGTON CARVER

As You Sow, So Shall You Reap.

BIBLICAL PROVERB

Appendix: Professional Tools

The CIBIC Professional Tools Library (PTL) includes seven assessment and development tools that are designed to promote the pursuit of excellence. The Mission and Objective Summary Table (MOST) is used to identify mission elements and their supporting objectives in a manner that promotes the identification of gaps and chaotic realities. The Chaos and Gap Examination (CAGE) worksheet is used to itemize the mission-impeding gaps and chaotic realities in a manner that promotes their direct resolution using the inner drivers and outer qualities. The Inner Driver Survey (IDS) is a flexible element survey designed to measure the strength of the nine inner drivers and their 36 subfactors in a manner that promotes expanded interpretation. The Inner Driver Peer Review (IDR) is a flexible element survey designed to measure the strength of the nine inner drivers and their 36 subfactors using unbiased feedback from peers, associates, clients, and family members among others. The Inner Driver Synopsis highlights the results of the inner driver survey using a visually dynamic circular format to promote later application and use. The Required Expectations Summary (REX) is designed to itemize prevailing goal-promoting expectations in a manner that promotes active development and full comprehension. The Driver and Quality Maximization Worksheet (MAX) is designed to highlight the inner drivers and outer qualities in a manner that promotes active development. The Subfactor Development Worksheet (SDW) is designed to promote the development of your critical subfactors through focused effort. The Change Initiating Procedure (CHIP) is designed to highlight the specific corrective actions that will promote desired goal-driven change. And finally, the CIBIC Master Worksheet is designed to promote the pursuit of excellence through direct gap management and planned resolution efforts. Together, these seven professional tools help to promote the awareness, preparation, and change that is synonymous with the pursuit of excellence and continuous improvement. Although not included in this library, the Cognitive Dynamics Sphere also promotes the pursuit of excellence, albeit in a nontabulated manner. By embracing the CIBIC professional tools library, CIBIC enthusiasts and CIBIC practitioners individually and collectively elevate their diligent pursuit of continuous improvement to a higher level. This pursuit, when promoted ad infinitum, can promote and perpetuate the pursuit of excellence. The CIBIC Professional Tools Library is available from CIBIC Incorporated in both printed and electronic formats for easy use and application.

Professional tools

MOST
Mission and objective
summary tabulation

CAGE
Chaos and gap elimination
worksheet

IDS
Inner driver survey

REX
Required expectations
summary

MAX
Driver and quality
maximization worksheet

CHIP
Change initiating profile

CIBIC TOOL 0 071717

CIBIC

Outer Strength From Inner Power

CIBIC MASTER WORKSHEET (CMW)

The CIBIC Master Worksheet is used to highlight your specific goals, gaps, and barriers in a manner that promotes their attainment or resolution using the critical facilitators, promoters, and accelerators. By highlighting your current realities and orchestrating your resolution elements, the CIBIC Master Worksheet helps you to promote a better tomorrow by helping you to exceed the prevailing expectations that exist, making continuous improvement a much easier endeavor.

NAME OR ORGANIZATION

GOAL # ___:

GAPS		COMMENT	BARRIERS		COMMENT
☐	SOCIAL		☐	NONCHALANCE	
☐	ECONOMIC		☐	NAIVETE	
☐	ENVIRONMENTAL		☐	DEVIANCE	
☐	PHYSIOLOGICAL		☐	MISSING COMPETENCIES	
☐	PSYCHOLOGICAL		☐	BIASES	
☐	BIO-CHEM-PHARMA		☐	SYSTEMIC FACTORS (CHAOS)	
☐	CHRONOLOGICAL		☐	UNCERTAINTY	
☐	PERFORMANCE		☐	MALAISE	
☐	TECHNICAL		☐	COERCION	
☐	SYSTEMIC CONSIDERATIONS (CHAOS)		☐	MISINFORMATION	
☐	OTHER	TRAUMA, DRAMA, PROBLEMS, SCANDALS	☐	FEAR	

RESOLUTION ELEMENTS (FACILITATORS & ACCELERATORS)

FACILITATORS (DO THESE EXIST?)			ACCELERATORS (HAVE THESE BEEN SUCCESSFULLY EMBRACED?)		
☐	VALUES		☐	EXCELLENCE	
☐	VISION		☐	EFFICIENCY	
☐	PRINCIPLES		☐	SUSTAINABILITY	
☐	PRACTICES		☐	VERSATILITY	
☐	PHILOSOPHIES		☐	QUALITY	
☐	IMAGINATION		☐	SYNERGIES	
☐	INGINUITY		☐	OTHER (COMMENT)	
☐	ORIGINALITY		☐	OTHER (COMMENT)	

C I B I C Continuous Improvement System Process

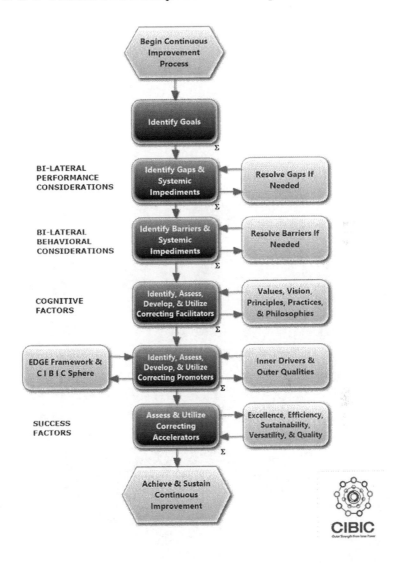

Glossary

acronymization: The use of acronyms to enhance learning and concept retention.

antagonist: Factor that corrupts and disrupts an otherwise favorable pursuit.

chaos: Unfavorable general circumstances and realities.

CHIP: A professional tool that promotes change management and change planning.

CIBIC: Acronym for continuous improvement by improving continuously.

cognitive dynamics sphere: A complex visual tool that highlights the connection between inner and outer attributes.

collective: Considerations involving teams, groups, organizations, and institutions.

COMPOSITE: Acronym that describes the nine outer qualities.

configuration: The process of aligning outer qualities to meet or exceed the prevailing expectations that exist.

continuation: The process of sustaining change and any other change-promoting activity.

CREAM: Acronym that describes the five change motions: coordination, resolution, execution, acquisition, and management.

deployment: The physical use of resources, including people, resources, and machinery to promote a given pursuit.

development: The process of acquiring or refining inner drivers and outer qualities to meet prevailing expectations.

discovery: The process of acquiring raw information and data from an exposure event.

DNA: Referring to inner drivers and outer qualities possessed by individuals or collective interests.

EDGE: Acronym for Efficiency and Detailed Gap Elimination; the basic system for continuous improvement.

elegance: The practice of embracing harmony to promote a given end pursuit.

expectations: A given set of tangible and intangible requirements for achieving good standing.

exposure: Basic access to people, experiences, and resources.

FACET: Acronym for focus, approach, commitment, expectations, and timing; five attributes of change.

FIRM diagram: Acronym for Freeman Intuitive Radial Measurement, a visual tool for representing inner driver strength.

framework: A system for achieving a chosen end result. Typically refers to the EDGE framework.

gaps: Objective- and goal-based deficiencies. Often a gateway enabler of chaos and chaotic realities.

GRASP: Acronym for Gap Responsibility, Accountability, Solvability, and Preventability.

HERD: Acronym for habit, engagement, reward, and dependency; four elements of reinforcement.

human factors: Relating to human resource development and utilization.

individual: Relating to the pursuits of a single person.

inner driver survey: A survey and assessment for measuring the strength of the nine inner drivers.

inner drivers: The nine inner attributes that promote the pursuit of excellence and continuous improvement.

insight: The knowledge and expertise gained from a given exposure event.

intonation: The use of tones or sounds to promote and reinforce learning and development.

ISO: Acronym for International Organization for Standardization, an international quality standards organization.

Kaizen: A Japanese business philosophy that promotes the continuous improvement of working practices and personal efficiency.

Lean: A systematic method for reducing waste and inefficiency in manufacturing and business processes.

level one: Very basic sequence of EDGE framework progressions.

level two: Summary sequence of EDGE framework progressions.

level three: Actionable sequence of EDGE framework progressions.

MAX: CIBIC professional tool that promotes the development of inner drivers and outer qualities.

metrics: Involving the measurement and analysis of basic information

MOST: CIBIC professional tool that promotes mission and objective driven management and planning.

optimal: Achieving the best reasonable result or outcome.

outer qualities: The nine outer-facing attributes that promote the pursuit of excellence and continuous improvement.

paradigm A: Theory of expectations approach that recognizes overperformance from undercommitments.

paradigm Z: Theory of expectations approach that recognizes underperformance from overcommitments.

peer review: The independent validation of inner driver survey results using peer surveys.

professional tools: A portfolio of surveys, worksheets, and assessments designed to support the CIBIC system.

progression: An incremental and definitive EDGE framework step.

SAPPHIRES: Acronym that describes the nine inner drivers.

Six Sigma: A management technique intended to greatly reduce the probability or errors or defects.

subfactors: Finite components of each inner driver and outer quality.

theory X: Human motivational theory that embraces the notion that individuals are not inherently motivated to succeed.

theory Y: Human motivational theory that embraces the notion that individuals are inherently motivated to succeed.

three laws: The three CIBIC laws designed to promote excellence and continuous improvement.

visualization: The use of graphics and illustration to convey concepts and ideas.

Endnotes

1. From Douglas McGregor's Human Motivation and Management Theory.

   The Human Motivation and Management Theory developed by Douglas McGregor introduced the alternate Theory X and Theory Y progress-promoting dynamics. The Theory X dynamic is a progress-promoting philosophy that emphasizes the predominant use of strict supervision, strict penalties, and external rewards to promote the pursuit of a desired end results. Alternately, the Theory Y dynamic is a progress-promoting philosophy that recognizes and emphasizes the predominant use of id-driven self-motivation, forward vision, direct responsibility, and direct accountability to promote the pursuit of a desired end results. The Theory Z dynamic, which is not included in the original theory, recognizes the existence of a third dynamic in which laissez-faire or progress-abating malaise is embraced or allowed. CIBIC as a continuous improvement system is primarily intended for use in Theory Y environments where achievement, responsibility, and accountability are promoted and embraced. However, in situations where Theory X and Theory Z philosophies are prevalent, CIBIC can be used to support the transformation to a Theory Y environment or dynamic.

2. From W. Edwards Deming—*Quality, Productivity, and Competitive Position*, 1982.

3. From Tom Peters—*In Search of Excellence*, 1982.

Where Is It Written?

F. ALLEN DAVIS

Index